Performance Analysis:
Knowing What to Do and How

Dale Brethower, Ph.D.

HRD Press, Inc. • **Amherst** • **Massachusetts**
ISPI • **Silver Spring** • **Maryland**

Volume 2 of the *Defining and Delivering Successful Professional Practice—HPT in Action* series

Series Editors:

Roger Kaufman, Ph.D., CPT
Dale Brethower, Ph.D.
Richard Gerson, Ph.D., CPT

Published by:

HRD Press, Inc.
22 Amherst Road
Amherst, MA 01002
800-822-2801 (U.S. and
  Canada)
413-253-3488
413-253-3490 (fax)
www.hrdpress.com

International Society for
  Performance Improvement
1400 Spring Street
Suite 260
Silver Spring, MD 20910
301-587-8570
301-587-8573 (fax)
www.ispi.org

ISBN 978-1-59996-054-8

Production services by Jean Miller
Editorial services by Sally Farnham
Cover design by Eileen Klockars

Table of Contents

Acknowledgments and Credits

Who should I acknowledge to help the reader understand the foundations of my thinking and writing? Who should I acknowledge because he or she has added specific value to my understanding of performance improvement? Who should I acknowledge to cover the political bases?

Acknowledgements to help the reader understand: I owe major intellectual debts to people who have passed from this earthly scene: Professor B. F. Skinner who sponsored my first professional paper and from whom I learned more than I learned from any other human being, except for my parents and my brothers; Professor S.S. Stevens who drove home important lessons about measurement; Professor G. S. Odiorne who modeled getting it done in the business world and whose wit and example made a lasting impression on many who knew him; Professor R.J. Herrnstein who taught me to look at experiments from the perspective of the subjects in the experiments and whose colleague, C. A. Murray, taught the same lesson about experiments in social policy. I must also acknowledge two persons I have never met, Adam Smith and Thomas Sowell. Their writings have shown this psychologist where to look to understand the economic consequences of performance improvement. There are many others to whom I owe intellectual debts but their names are not as readily recognized as the names above. I am thankful that Murray and Sowell are still with us and that the others live on through their works.

Acknowledgements of specific value added to my understanding: a comprehensive and honest list would be quite long; it would include dozens of colleagues and clients and hundreds of students. Deciding just who should be on the list would give me a headache. Please let me prevent the headache by beginning and ending with just one name: Geary Rummler. Geary, a friend and colleague for 40 years or so, is the best I know at expanding the frontiers of our understanding by constantly looking for the important variables that influence performance and constantly figuring out better ways to manage those variables.

Acknowledgements to cover political bases: political acknowledgements would be totally out of character for me, but there is one name I must mention because not doing so would be silly. Not because of political correctness, Roger Kaufman would hoot at that. But because Roger has steadfastly focused on strategic issues in a way that should be enlightening for all. As he might say, "If performance improvement is the solution, what is the problem?" or "If strategy is the solution, what is the problem?" or "If survival is the solution, what is the problem?" or "If competence is the solution, what is the problem?" What is the problem? The problem is that entropy tends to increase. Disorganization abounds in the social and commercial worlds. If we are not organizing our efforts to improve performance now and later, for us and for them, we are at least as likely to make things worse as we are to make things better. That is worth acknowledging, is it not?

Dale Brethower
April, 2006

Preface
What the Divers of Le Quebrada, Executives, and Managers Have in Common

Executives are similar to the divers who dive off the high cliffs at Le Quebrada (near Acapulco, Mexico). We are impressed with the divers' performance because we know that failure is a possibility and can be deadly. The divers are experts who make the difficult seem easy. So, too, are executives who attend to the right variables to influence performance.

The divers do at least one thing that you and I could do: They stand high on the cliff and look down. If we did that, we would see what the divers see, but we could not do what the divers do next. The divers watch the water to time the dive properly so that they hit the water as a wave rolls in, and not a second later when the wave rolls out again. They might not understand the physics involved, but they respect the waves. They dive. They feel the adrenaline rush. The water rushes in. They catch the wave and the wave catches them. They survive and dive again another day. Executives who properly time entry into a market survive to work another day.

What the diver sees is not what you and I would see, even if we were standing where the diver stands. We would see exactly the same view—the same surface features of the water and wind and rocks and waves. But you and I would not see what the diver sees, "in his mind's eye." The diver sees beyond the surface. The diver sees the current state of important variables. The diver sees what some call the "deep structure."

The deep structure is a set of principles that support the waves and a few indicators that the diver observes. Deep structure principles explain the surface structure, but the diver doesn't care. He just wants to time his dive perfectly. He can do so by observing a few key indicators. He might not even consciously know what those key indicators are, having learned them by experience from associating with other successful divers. Ask a diver how he knows when to dive and he'll tell you he just knows; it comes from experience.

Executives and managers learn their trades much the way the divers of Le Quebrada learn theirs. Executives and managers typically have more schooling than do the divers. If the diver went to school, however, it would not be one taught by someone who had never dived *and* who never closely analyzed what successful divers do.

The performance analyst helps executives and managers see the deep structure of performance. We analyze success and identify deep structure variables that support success.

Our task is difficult because it is much easier to define success for the divers of Le Quebrada than for executives or managers. A successful executive or manager might have been lucky enough to "catch the wave" a time or two. A diver might do so a time or two as well, but not many times unless he had become expert. A successful diver is easy to identify: He is alive after many dives.

A successful manager or executive? He or she has "dived" a time or two and caught a wave of attention of writers of management books and articles. But check the bookshelves over the past five years or so. How many companies have taken a dive? How many have taken a dive after the executive or manager had been declared a success by authors hungry for a story to sell?

Our task as performance analysts is not quite as dangerous and it is a bit more complex than helping the divers of Le Quebrada. But from the 50,000-foot level, it is exactly the same task:

We help people get in touch with just the right deep structure variables to yield the surface structure results they seek.

Or would seek, if they just knew about those potential results.

Our task, as performance analysts, is to help executives and managers and knowledge workers and skilled laborers and unskilled laborers improve performance. We do not do the work ourselves. We do not pull the barge or lift the bale. We help performers do the work. Performers must know which barge to pull, where to pull it, what bales to carry, and much more. That is where we come in: We are improvers of performance-at-work—improvers of organizational and process and individual performance.

I will try to make analysis of organizational performance look easy in this book. It is never easy in reality, but I'll try to make it seem that way—not to fool you, but to be as clear as possible. Parts that will be easy for some readers will be difficult for others. I apologize for the difficulties and hope you understand that an author can only write as clearly as possible and make guesses about your questions and concerns.

The book is in three sections and contains eight chapters. Each section has an overview to help you know what issues it deals with. There is a glossary of terms that contains words that I (and the authors of the other books in this series) have agreed to use as defined therein. Readers might also find it useful to use one or more of the Internet search engines to get more information about the concepts (including concepts not in the glossary). For example, you might do a search on "subsystem maximization" or some other term that catches your interests. (I recommend using the quotation marks because it keeps the searches better focused than searches without them).

I have done my best to write clearly. If you do your best to read intelligently, success is (almost) assured.

System Thinking: A Way of Looking at Performance Issues

System Thinking: Converting Confusion into Clarity

When we successfully analyze an organizational problem, we convert uncertainty or confusion into clarity about actions to take. Before an analysis, there are competing ideas.

Example 1:

"Sales are down because of the recession."

"Sales are down because too few of our salespeople are competent."

"Sales are down because of a seasonal slump that we always have about now."

"Sales are down because too many of our products are on the down leg of the product life cycle."

"Sales are down because the numbers were wrong earlier; what we are now seeing are the right numbers."

"Sales are down because our competitors just brought out a hot new line of products."

Example 2:

"Our scrap rate is too high and our shipped quality is too low because our quality assurance people are too slow and use antiquated test instruments."

"Our quality is too low because we've just hired several new people and the training department didn't do a good job of training them.

"Our quality is too low because purchasing has tried to save a few dollars by buying materials that do not meet our quality standards."

"Our quality is just fine. We are measuring things the customers do not care about. It would be a waste of money to try to fix something that isn't broken."

Before the analysis, we experience the confusion and disagreement about actions to take. There are well-intentioned but quite different ideas about what to do. The analysis enables us to see the causes of the confusion a bit more clearly, verify the existence of the problem, and identify one or more things to do about it.

The newly discovered clarity enables us to move forward and learn more. If we learn enough of the right things and act on them, we succeed much more often than not. If we act too slowly, too quickly, or in ignorance, we succeed much less often. Analyzing organizations competently increases our chances of success.

I like to describe the pre-analysis confusion as a "booming-buzzing confusion" and the goal as "converting the booming-buzzing confusion into booming-buzzing clarity." I owe the "booming-buzzing" metaphor to the great American philosopher, William James. It describes what we do in life, in analyzing problems, and in leading people.

James described the experience of the new-born child as a booming-buzzing confusion. The child has a few wired-in predispositions, but nothing in the newborn's world is familiar, already experienced, or something the child already knows how to deal with.

The child gradually learns to navigate the booming-buzzing confusion by learning "what leads to what." Sucking on some things makes the child feel better; sucking on others does not. And so it goes throughout life: Doing some things makes the person feel or function better; doing other things does not. Doing some things helps a person understand how to deal with complex problems; doing other things does not.

It is the same in leading and managing an organization: Doing some things helps the people and the organization work better; doing other things does not. A good analysis helps us do the right things better or faster or cheaper; a bad analysis does not.

Leaders and managers set the tone for an organization and strongly influence key performance variables. If we are to help leaders and managers improve performance, we should understand the variables influencing the performance of interest *and* the variables influencing leaders and managers.

The Major Task of Leadership

The major task of leadership is to ensure that people move from booming-buzzing confusion to booming-buzzing clarity. The booming-buzzing confusion issue that is central to leadership is confusion about the future:

- Should we launch a new product?
- Acquire another firm?
- Merge?
- Sell?
- Should we develop a different product line?
- Enter a new market?
- Focus on our competitive edge, if we can figure out just what it is?

As we look back in history, we see leaders grappling with a booming-buzzing confusion.

For example, think back to what you know about what was happening in the world just before World War II. Different leaders had different ideas about what actions to take. Leaders in Germany and Japan believed the thing to do was to conquer; leaders in the United States and Great Britain believed the thing to do was to resist. Many citizens in all four nations disagreed with their own leaders and, at least in the United States and Great Britain, vehemently and publicly disagreed.

The task of leadership in all four nations was to create an agreed-upon clarity of action. That is the major task of leadership of a nation or a company or a department or a family.

The Major Task of Management

The major task of management is different than the major task of leadership. Once leaders clarify direction, correctly or incorrectly, the major task of management becomes doing what it takes to follow the lead. An additional task of management is providing leaders with information about whether the direction is correct or incorrect.

For example, once leaders took our nation into World War II or the Vietnam War or the Gulf War, it was the task of management to guide efforts to win the war. Military management became very important. Generals and admirals and such took the actions that guided thousands of (up until then) ordinary citizens to take action. The actions, eventually, decide which nations emerge as the winners and which emerge as the losers, and which individuals are casualties and which are survivors.

The military managers spent great sums, in money and materials and lives. War, even perceived with the clarity of hindsight, remains a booming-buzzing confusion. The examples of World War II, a "police action" or two since then, and the war on terror illustrate two important points:

1. Leading is directed toward the future. Leaders cannot be sure about what they are doing; nevertheless, the consequences of their decisions are huge.

2. Managers do not decide direction, but have to know what they are doing if we are to get there.

Leaders, in an important sense:

- Cannot know what they are doing *and*
- Must persuade others to follow them anyway.

Leaders must look at the booming-buzzing confusion that surrounds them and lead people to make sense of it—to a shared clarity of what should be done.

Managers, on the other hand, should know what they are doing. Managers' responsibilities can be described in terms of what Albert Ellis,[1] the therapist, calls "conditional should."

- "If this is our goal, here is what we should do…"
- "If we go after an increased market share for this product, here is what we should do…"
- "If we decide to save the plant in Philadelphia, here is what we should do…"
- "If we decide to build a hybrid gasoline and electric car, here is what we should do…"
- "If government policy is to develop alternative energy sources right now, here is what we should do…"
- "If the goal is to bring about a better life for children throughout the world, here is what we should do…"

Or, as Albert Ellis might state a conditional should in his line of work: "If you want to stop acting like a nutty person, here is what you should do..." In Ellis's thinking, "shoulds" are always conditional—dependent on a specific set of conditions.

The performance analyst might state a conditional "should" this way: "If you want to have specific performance results, here is what you should do...." A therapist such as Albert Ellis cannot tell you what your goals in life should be, now and forever; a performance analyst cannot tell you what your organizational goals should be. But we can tell you that your goals should be clear, consistent, and measured, now and forever. We can help.

Leaders look at confusing situations and say: "This is what we should do!" Managers look at confusing situations and say: "If X is our goal, this is what we should do...."

Leaders are more persuasive if they say why: "X is our goal and here is why....!" Managers are more persuasive if they set up management systems so that everyone knows "What I should do, why, how, when, how well, and with whom."

That is it! You now know the tasks of leaders and of managers. Leadership is about where we should go; management is about how we could get there. An expert in performance improvement must help them do their tasks if he or she is to help them improve performance. Seems obvious, doesn't it? But many of us, allegedly in the performance improvement business, begin toting barges and lifting bales without doing the analysis necessary to establish a clear notion of where the barge is going or why or when it must arrive. Or worse, we tote barges and lift bales without a clue about the organizational consequences of our work.

Continue reading this book if you would like some of the details—details about figuring out what to do and how, about getting fallible human beings to agree, and getting fallible human beings (including yourself) to act intelligently.

About System Thinking

This book applies and is a product of system thinking. System thinking is a way of looking at the world—a perspective that is common among successful farmers, naval admirals, parents, and a few great leaders and managers.

System thinking looks at anything that performs as a system. All these are systems:

- A small business
- A not-for-profit agency
- My neighbor's dog
- A fallible human being (who might be the owner/operator/ janitor of a small business or a professional in a not-for-profit agency)
- A rose bush
- A family
- An ecosystem
- Your favorite aunt

This book will not talk about rose bushes, aunts, and dogs, but will use examples of the other systems to help you understand system concepts. The idea is to help you ground them *in your experience* so that you do not have to take my word about relevance and applicability.

The four chapters in Section I describe and illustrate system analysis as a way to figure out what to do and why.

Chapter 1: System Analysis: Attaining Clarity of Direction opens the way, discussing the importance of gathering information about context and searching for critical issues faced by the organization and its people.

Chapter 2: The Systemic Thinking Lens continues the discussion of systemic context and finding the variables that impact performance. The chapter points out some variables that can be managed and some that cannot. The chapter introduces fundamental systemic concepts, describing the concepts in the context of a business and in the context of a family. Why in the context of a family? Two reasons: First, all readers have experience in at least one family; second, some businesses, especially not-for-profits, serve families and like to think they create a family atmosphere within the business.

Chapter 3: Systems Analysis of a Business goes into more detail, showing seven different views (others might call them seven perspectives or areas of emphasis). The chapter is about how the different views interact and how they would work in a specific business. The views are:

1. The system perspective: how we fit into the world out there (Mega, Macro, Micro)

2. The anatomy of performance perspective: the world we connect to

3. The performance system perspective: the minimum set of variables to support intelligent performance (total performance system, mission statement)

4. The value-adding processes: the primary processes that perform the work necessary to add value

5. The support processes: the necessary work that supports primary processes

6. The performers: the human performance system variables necessary to support their work

7. The management processes: such as measurable objectives and performance criteria

Chapter 4: Systems Analysis of a Family shows the same seven views, illustrating a system view of a family. The family is used for two reasons. First, we are all reasonably familiar with what a family is and how a family functions, both well and poorly. Second, there has been a great deal of work on the family-as-system, work that some readers might want to refer to later to learn about it in depth.

If you reflect on your experiences in organizations and in families, you will understand exactly why the chapters focus on two very different types of variables:

- "Variables that I can control that are necessary, but not sufficient to do the job"

- "Variables that are out of my control, but that I must attend to"

The argument is that, in a system, everything is connected to everything else; consequently, a performance analyst must examine *many* connections. Why? To ensure that the performance improvement interventions used will actually improve performance and not be overwhelmed by homeostatic "resistance," the tendency of a system to remain stable, and to ensure that interventions will not go forward when the critical performance variables cannot be changed.

Endnote

1. The conditional should is a very useful concept introduced by Albert Ellis, the founder of Rational Emotive Behavioral Therapy (see http://rebt-cbt.net/ for more information about REBT). The notion is that therapists and scientists and consultants are unwise to attempt to tell clients what they *should* do in any absolute sense. A performance improvement consultant might say, "If you want to pursue that goal, here is what you should do..."or "Before you commit to that goal, here are some things you might consider...."Our science and technology enable us to speak authoritatively about the variables necessary to support performance, but our science and technology does not enable us to speak in absolute terms about the goal. Should an organization pursue a specific strategic goal or not? We cannot dictate the answer, but we can help leaders understand the costs and consequences of a course of action.One of the strengths of Kaufman's Organizational Elements Model described in Book One of this series is that it helps leaders decide about the "shoulds" so that their organizations help, rather than hinder, the creation of a better future for all.

Chapter 1
System Analysis: Attaining Clarity of Direction

Overview: Getting Better Results

Chapter 1 shows tactics that a performance analyst can use to help attain clarity of direction for a performance improvement project. The analyst reads, listens actively, and organizes information to help clients understand what to do, why, and how.

- The "why" is always to get better results.

- The "what" and "how" always involve trying something and learning from the experience.

This book and this chapter are about discovering why, what, and how:

- How do the analyst and the client and the project team know what results are worth working for?

- How do they know what to try first and second and third, and how do they know when and where to try them?

- How do they track the effects of their efforts to keep the efforts on track toward the results?

The process typically begins with a request or by noticing an opportunity. The process requires tenacious pursuit of answers to fundamental questions. Illustrative questions are:

- What is the direction (the mission, the goals, the strategy) of the organization?

- What is working well?

- What should be improved?

- Why? (And why? And why? And why?)

- What is going on in the organization that will help the effort? That will hinder or compete with the effort?

- Who are the key players?

- If the project is a success, what will success look like?

- How will stakeholders (inside and outside the organization) benefit?

Answers, by themselves, create a clutter of disorganized data.

The analyst must organize the data so that it can guide decisions that, when implemented, improve performance.

The analysis of the data uses practical procedures readily comprehended by intelligent businesspeople. It does not use esoteric procedures that are incomprehensible except to researchers. The questioning procedures and the data organization procedures are guided by what we know about organizations-as-systems and what we know about the specific organization.

We do not seek simply to change performance; we seek to improve it. Improving it is a much more difficult and much more valuable task than merely changing performance.

The analysis procedures should be guided by the Certification Standards put forth by the International Society for Performance Improvement[1] (ISPI). The 10 standards, say ISPI thought leaders, must be met to demonstrate competence in performance improvement work.

The analysis procedures focus on adding measured value, collaboratively, in the context of the functioning total organization. Improving a part can harm the whole, just as surely as aggressively cutting costs can harm production, profitability, and customer satisfaction; making small improvements in existing products can harm strategic positioning for new products in new markets; or improving short-term profits can harm long-term prospects for success.

Finding direction for performance improvement requires asking the right questions, tenaciously, to:

- Get information about the context in which the effort will occur

- Search for critical issues facing the organization and the people in it

- Convert the data into information

- Organize the information so that it can be linked directly to action

Gather Information about Context

Attaining clarity of direction for a human performance improvement project is easier than attaining clarity of direction for an entire organization, but only if organization direction is already clear. If the organization direction is fuzzy, even a clear and agreed-upon direction for a project may be going in exactly the wrong direction.

TIPS FOR ANALYSIS

That is just the way it is—and one reason that it is wise to use every performance improvement project as an opportunity to clarify and confirm organizational direction.

Sometimes the organization has recently clarified its mission. Perhaps the mission is to do many wonderful things, including deliver X value-adding goods and services to customers in market segment Y.

A sharply focused statement of direction is a big help. For example, consider this mission statement:

Acme Home Landscaping provides landscaping services to builders and buyers that add attractiveness to fine homes, thereby enhancing the beauty and the economy of the neighborhood.

Please notice something about this mission statement. It speaks to value to be added beyond the walls of Acme Home Landscaping. The mission statements I use and recommend answer the question: What value do we add, to whom, where, and how? Mission statements can be quite lofty, spelling out the intention to make the world a better place. And why not? Why not strive to make the world a better place by helping clients add value?

Mission statements, goal statements, advertising brochures, and similar documents are a good starting point for analysis because they help the analyst get clear about the context of the improvement effort. This is especially true if the analyst clarifies and confirms by asking many people, "What does it mean to you?"

Anyone wishing to help Acme improve performance should create or confirm a clear starting point. That is why many consulting firms include a brief situation analysis in proposals. It confirms the starting point and shows that the consultants can listen, think, organize, and write clearly and succinctly. It only takes a little background information and a little business sense for an analyst to generate several hypotheses (to correct or confirm) about almost any firm, including Acme:

- What is Acme's market segment?
  Hypothesis to test: Builders and buyers of upscale homes, probably custom homes (if you prefer plain language, just say "analyst's guess" wherever I say "Hypothesis to test")

- What is their value promise to customers?
  Hypothesis to test: Acme promises to enhance the beauty and economic value of fine homes.

- What is Acme's competitive strategy?
  Hypothesis to test: Acme competes on quality of the work completed and on the economic value added. Acme does not compete on price.

- How does Acme market?
  Hypotheses to test: Acme probably markets through builder's associations, maybe homeowner's associations, possibly through real estate agents catering to the fine home buyer and seller, and almost certainly through word of mouth. Marketing brochures are likely to show Acme's landscaping work and the neighborhoods the landscaped homes are in.

One trip to Acme headquarters and brief and casual conversations with people there might be enough to test the hypotheses. Why test them? To confirm, clarify, or change them. And to help the client keep the items meaningful.

The leadership of Acme would readily talk about their business and elaborate, clarify, confirm, and add detailed understanding. Getting the detailed understanding opens the door to more in-depth conversation, guided by leading questions. Analysts earn or lose trust by the questions we ask.

Search for Critical Issues Faced by the Organization and the People

Good questions lead the conversation toward important issues. An analyst knows from the outset that there will be three interconnected sets of issues:

1. The work of the business
2. The finances of the business
3. The people in the business

The following scenario illustrates how this part of the analysis might work. The questions asked are based on context information and the analyst's current and growing understanding of the work, the people, and the business. The analyst has done some homework before the interview.

John, how long have you been in business in this area?
(Asked only if it was not stated in a brochure or Yellow Pages ad.)

Do you do any commercial landscaping?
Possible answer: "Not really. I have a goal to landscape some of the builders' premises and a few of the realtors'. It is a form of advertising. We give them a price break if we can do it off-peak times. You know, to keep our crews busy a bit more of the time."

How is it that you can do such good work?
Possible answer: "My partner is a landscape architect. She is really good, but when I met her, she was struggling to make it on her own. Now she can concentrate on what she's good at and let me concentrate on the business aspects. It is a win for both of us."

I saw one of your projects on the way here. Your people seem to know what they are doing. (Pause)
Possible answer: "Some of the people we've had on-board for a while do. Cindy watches the others like a hawk! As well as being a great architect, she is a tough supervisor and great coach."

How important is it to get a project completed on time?
>   **Possible answer:** "Extremely! Otherwise our costs go up and our customers get really, really angry."

You probably get more than 90 percent of them done on time. (Pause)
>   **Possible answer:** "Yes. We do."

What is your on-time completion percentage?
>   **Possible answer:** "I don't know exactly. It is probably around 99 percent!"

Is that good compared to other landscapers in this market?
>   **Possible answer:** "Yes. We are the best!"

You must have to do a lot to keep on-time completion high. (Pause)
>   **Possible answer:** "That's for sure! I have to make sure we have crews available. That's a headache! I have to make sure we have trees and shrubs and flowers and rocks and irrigation equipment and everything else!"

But a lot of that is out of your control, isn't it? (Pause)
>   **Possible answer:** "You have that right!"

Can't you just explain to your customers that the delays aren't your fault? (Pause)
>   **Possible answer:** "My customers do not give a *#@! about that! They want it on time!"

What can you do about it, then?
>   **Possible answer:** "I carry a little extra inventory on key items. I persuade Cindy to do designs that give me a little flexibility about what plants we use. There are lots of little things. I just do what has to be done."

How do you do what has to be done without annoying your suppliers? (Pause)
>   **Possible answer:** "I do annoy them! I explain that I'm the customer and I want what I want when I want it, just like *my* customers do!"

You probably annoy some of them more than others.
Possible answer: "That's right! I'd like to fire some of them, but I can't find anyone better. I'm stuck with them. But the good news is they are stuck with me, too! They can't afford to lose me as a customer."

You must have a lot of expense in doing landscaping like you do. Do you finance it yourself, or do you borrow money?
Possible answer: "I finance it myself if I can. I do not like to use the line of credit if I do not have to. I do not want to max it out right in the midst of the busiest seasons."

No wonder Cindy had trouble with the business side! Does she appreciate all you do to make sure the projects get done properly?
Possible answer: "I'm lucky to have found her. She's been there, done that. Before she came onboard, I had hired two or three other landscape architects who were clueless."

Is that why Cindy is a partner, not an employee? You want to be sure she stays with the business?
Possible answer: "Yes."

You know, I really hope we can do a project with you. I really hate working with clients who are not good businesspeople. (Pause)
Possible answer: "I don't know how good I am, but I try. Why do you care, though? I'd think in your line of work you'd want to find businesses that weren't run very well."

Ask Cindy why we do not do that. She'll explain it to you if you ask her the right question: Why doesn't she plant things where they won't grow? Her answer will fit my business. I want to plant things where they will grow. If we help a poor businessperson, all we'll get is a fee. Our work will wither and die. We might get a referral, but we won't get repeat business. We just can't succeed by planting things where they won't grow! Cindy can tell you that.

TIPS FOR ANALYSIS
You might want to reread this scenario once or twice as you prepare to meet with a client such as a business owner, senior manager, or executive. As you read, ask yourself: "Why is that question being asked? How would an analyst know to ask it? If I ask that question, how should I phrase it?"

Standards for Performance Improvement Work

The International Society for Performance Improvement sponsored the development of standards for good work in our field. Many people were involved. The people represented a variety of educational backgrounds and had experience in a variety of for-profit and not-for-profit organizations. After careful consideration and much discussion, these exceptional individuals were able to summarize agreements about basic principles. They captured four of the most basic and important principles in four Standards for Certified Performance Technologists. The four standards are listed here, copied directly from the ISPI web site. The URL (in August 2006) is: http://www.certifiedpt.org/index.cfm?section=standards. The four standards are:

1. Focus on results and help clients focus on results.

2. Look at situations systemically, taking into consideration the larger context including competing pressures, resource constraints, and anticipated change.

3. Add value in how you do the work and through the work itself.

4. Utilize partnerships or collaborate with clients and other experts as required.

The four standards are interrelated and inseparable.

If you study the little analysis dialogue above with these standards in mind, you will discover the rationale for many, perhaps all, of the questions. The questioner is attempting to tease out the value to be added and the specific results that will help add value (Standards 3 and 1). The way the questions are asked emphasizes collaboration and positions the consultant as someone who seeks to work with the client to add value (Standard 4). The questions take into consideration "the larger context including competing pressures, resource constraints, and anticipated changes" (Standard 2). The questions have touched on business matters such as relationships with suppliers of tools, materials, money, people, sales and marketing leads, and—in Cindy's case at least—expertise. The questions shown have not probed about anticipated changes, but have positioned the analyst to ask about ongoing or anticipated innovations. For example, these questions would flow naturally:

Do you grow any of your own plants?

Do you have close relationships with really good nurseries?

What are some of the innovations you would like to make but haven't gotten to yet?

Did Cindy's contacts help you find customers? Good employees?

How important to developing and retaining good employees is the coaching Cindy does?

Notice that the questions—set up by answers to previous questions—give the analyst clues about how to design and position a proposal or just develop a relationship with a client. This is important whether the analyst is an external vendor or an internal manager or support person.

Please understand, also, that the analysis questions flow out of the dialogue, not out of a preconceived script. Some people like to have the analysis questions scripted, but I think that is usually a weak tactic. If the questions are scripted, the conversation tends to feel more like an interrogation than a collaboration. It takes enormous skill in scripting and in asking scripted questions to use that tactic well. Scripted and relatively inflexible questioning can be counterproductive simply because people tend to like to collaborate and dislike being interrogated.

TIPS FOR ANALYSIS

I often prepare a script to get ready for an interview. Sometimes I have it with me during the interview, but do not use it except, perhaps, as a checklist late in the interview. "Pardon me a second while I glance over my notes to see if we have covered all the questions I should have asked." I might end the interview that way, but my script often has this as the last question: "What else should I know?"

An analysis that wanders all over the place, following up on whatever the client says, wastes the client's time and does not consistently yield good information. An analyst with no more intellectual capacity than the average genius must have a way to keep the analysis simple, flexible, and productive. Keeping the four standards in mind does that. I use a collaborative style (Standard 4) and openly search for the potential for adding value (Standard 3). In addition, I try to ensure that the content of the questions probes potential systemic issues about relationships with customers, investors, suppliers, and employees (Standard 2). I also know a little about business, which helps in looking for results measures (Standard 1). I am not a business expert by training, but you and I and the client all know some of the important basics:

- The employees do the work.

- The goods and services should benefit the customers.

- Good relationships with the suppliers—including the suppliers of cash, capital, technology, and potential employees—are essential.

Clients like to get value for their money. That's why I seek to focus on results (Standard 1) that we will measure to assure the client (and me) that the value-added we sought (Standard 3) actually comes out of our work.

The Analyst's "Mental Model"

The mental model for the analyst *should include these four standards,* which capture the collective wisdom of the ISPI members who developed the standards. An individual analyst's mental model will, of course, be augmented by any tools and experiences the analyst has available. The augmentation can be very helpful, but it can also be very counterproductive. It will be helpful if the tools and experience help get information about all four standards; it will be counterproductive if it supports a drift away from the standards.

Any performance improvement project can and should be guided by the four standards. It not only clarifies matters for the client, it also helps those of us doing performance improvement projects to build on what one another does.

Think about it: If we seek to improve the performance of a not-for-profit agency:

- Would we (deliberately) set out to improve a performance that does not add value to clients or employees or funding agencies, or to the larger society?

- Wouldn't we like to improve the performance of the agency as a whole and do so without sacrificing any part?

- Wouldn't we prefer a project that benefits as many stakeholders as possible and harms none?

- Wouldn't we like to communicate clearly about what we do?

If we seek to improve the performance of a for-profit organization:

- Would we deliberately set out to improve a performance that does not add value to clients or employees or investors or the larger society?

- Wouldn't we like to improve the performance of the organization as a whole and do so without sacrificing any part?

- Wouldn't we prefer a project that benefits as many stakeholders as possible and harms none?

- Wouldn't we like to communicate clearly about what we do?

If you want to be sure that a project, program, or ongoing operation is beneficial, it must meet all four standards! Seek not a direction that fails to meet the standards!

The four standards define the value promise for a project and for our field. We promise to get measured results that consider organizational reality, add value, and do so by working collaboratively with the people involved. We seek win-win results, not win-lose results.

The four standards are quite specific, yet they apply to any performance improvement effort, including an effort to improve the performance of a racing car! Think about it. Would a racing team set out to "improve" a car's performance in a way that does not add value (Standard 3)? That does not lead to a measured result (Standard 1)? That improves performance of some little thing about the race car, but detracts from overall performance (Standard 2)? And is any one person so expert in everything there is to know about race cars that he or she can do it all, without collaborating with other experts (Standard 4)? Successful race teams might not know the four standards, but you can be sure that they "apply" them!

One of the nice things about the four standards is that customers can understand them right away. It is easy to explain what each standard means, using examples and terms used by the people in a specific business. That done, just ask: "Would you knowingly hire a consultant who did not work to these four standards?" Or ask: "Would you want the company to spend money on an internal consultant who does not work to these four standards?"

These four standards define the essence of our field in a very practical way. It would be extremely foolish to ignore them, especially while seeking to define the scope and direction for a performance improvement project.

Convert the Data to Information

A typical analysis generates a great deal of data. By "data" I mean everything from confirmed numbers to anecdotes, rumors, unsupported opinions, and vague impressions of who is or is not trustworthy. Client impressions of the analyst are also important data and should be collected, at least informally. Some of the data will be useless, confusing, misleading, or inaccurate. Some of the unsupported opinions will turn out to be important, once they are supported. But none of the data will be useful unless they are converted into information.

By "converted into information" I mean clarified and confirmed and arranged so that the data support specific action plans. Facts are data. Information comes from linking data to action. It is extremely important to organize the data so that it informs and guides potential actions, such as: follow six recommendations, authorize someone to take action, hire the analyst's firm, sell a division, discontinue a product line.

The way the data are organized and presented is extremely important. Think of what you do to present the data to the client as if it is an instructional communication. It is! You are presenting a lesson that has specific instructional objectives. The results of the analysis should be presented in a way that allows the client to learn from it, correct inaccuracies, confirm accuracies, fill in blanks, and discuss implications.

Here is a checklist for evaluating the presentation. The presentation should help clients:

1. Focus on results.

2. Look at situations systemically, taking into consideration the larger context including competing pressures, resource constraints, and anticipated change.

3. Add value in the actions they take and in how they take action.

4. Utilize partnerships or collaborate with others in the organization, other experts, or other stakeholders as required.

Think about it: If these criteria are not met, the project is likely to be a waste of resources, is it not?

Some consultants write reports as if they were writing a textbook. The report is detailed, technically accurate, comprehensive, and destined to be forgotten very soon. Please do not do it that way! You add value by providing guidance for actions that improve specific performance.

There is a proven model for the presentation. The model is the research seminar. It might surprise you to know that, but consider this: Research seminars deal in "results to date," support interactions among peers, and yield two things—shared understanding and plans for further research. Presenting the results of an analysis focused on performance improvement should have one more yield, for a total of three. It should yield:

1. Shared understanding
2. Plans for further research
3. Plans for practical action

Why "plans for further research"? Because no analysis yields all the information a client could ask for. Clients and researchers can always think of something else they would like to know, even if it is "How can I refute some of these findings?"

Instructional designers can tell you that a presentation with such (generic) objectives must be interactive, guided, and collaborative, and have means of capturing ideas, agreements, and uncertainties. It must move toward a consensus about three things:

1. What we agree on
2. What additional information and support we want
3. Action plans for next steps

Clients understand the logic to this presentation model. It does not have to be explained. They know that "What we agree on" is the foundation for "next steps." They know that disconnected bits of data are abundant, whereas information and resources are limited. It will be obvious to them that they must figure out how to get the additional information and resources.

TIPS FOR ANALYSIS

If someone tells you that clients are "resistant to analysis" or "won't pay for analysis," you can be sure the speaker is not talking about projects that *collaborate* with clients in this way.

Organize the Information to Link to Action Steps

"Information maps,"[2] "intellectual scaffolding,"[3] "models," "simple graphics," and "KISS" are all terms that describe techniques and guidelines intended to enable people to "connect the dots" and understand complexity. A picture is indeed worth a thousand or so words, especially if it is a picture that describes how to obtain desired results.

Consulting firms typically have favored graphics, almost trade-marks, that they use to organize their messages. I mention this because trademarks are typically designed to capture an idea and show it simply.

My favorite, almost-a-personal-trademark[4,5] graphic is shown in Figure 1.1, summarizing information about Acme Landscaping.

Figure 1.1: Acme Landscaping

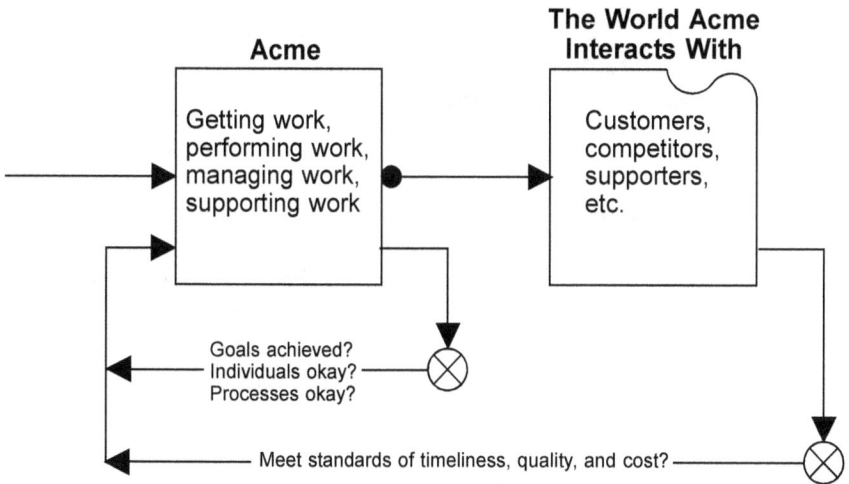

Goal Statement: Acme Home Landscaping provides landscap-ing services to builders and buyers that add attractiveness to fine homes, thereby enhancing the beauty and the economy of the neighborhood.

I might use the graphic in talking to John and Cindy:

Dale: I use this picture to keep the big picture of Acme in focus. There are so many important things to know about what you do that it is easy for me to get lost in the detail. Does that ever happen to you? Do you get so wrapped up in details that you can forget what is really important?

Cindy: That is why I came to work for John. I liked the land-
         scaping, but all the business and financial details just
         confused me. I can keep all the details of a landscap-
         ing project in my head, but I can't keep the whole
         business in my head!

John: I think that's why I do my best thinking late at night or
         early in the morning. I can set the details aside and
         concentrate on what's important!

Dale: Is it frustrating to either of you that the employees
         sometimes do things that show they just do not under-
         stand what is going on?

John: Yes!

Cindy: I get really annoyed sometimes. I won't mention any
         names, but there are a couple of people who just don't
         get it. I really have to watch them closely. I tell them
         what we are doing in a project and they nod their
         heads and even tell me what I've told them. But later
         in the day, they do something that shows they must
         have forgotten all about it.

Dale: I hope I don't do that very often when I'm working with
         you two! This picture helps me. It might even be useful
         to you at some point. Let me show it to you and ask
         some questions to make sure it is accurate.

Here are some of the questions I might ask:

- Does the way I've written the mission statement seem
  about right? Would you say it differently?

- Is the description of your major customers and prospects
  about right?

- Cindy, does this internal feedback loop capture some of
  the information you use to guide projects?

- John, does this external feedback loop capture some of
  the information you use?

- Notice that the input arrow refers to new projects, and the output arrow refers to completed projects. Does that make sense to you?

- John, the diagram focuses on the work. It doesn't show the flow of money into and out of Acme Landscaping. That is important, isn't it? You have to have a clear picture of the money flow, do you not?

If John and Cindy are actively engaged and we are clarifying the picture, I ask the questions and make notes. As soon as they are not engaged, I set it aside and go on to something else. (I might come back to it a day or so later if we encounter an issue that it might help clarify.)

Another tool I might use is the role matrix shown in Figure 1.2. It organizes data in a way that might help clarify John's leader/owner role and Cindy's manager/partner role.

Here is a segment of how the discussion might go:

Dale: Please take a look at this matrix. It shows how I am piecing things together at the moment. Look it over and ask anything you want.

John: Okay. I'm not sure how to look at this thing. Where do I look first?

Dale: Just look at John's role and especially at the key questions. Is it important that you are able to answer questions like that?

John: Yes. Those questions are about strategy. Strategic issues are on my plate.

Cindy: I know John is always pushing me to improve profit margins! And he keeps telling me we have to get ready to handle more work.

Dale: Then we'd better pencil that in! Put it in the box with your measures. Just add "Profit Margins" to that box.

John: I push Cindy on profit margins, but a lot of that is out of her control, especially when I don't get enough input from her when I bid on a job.

Figure 1.2: Organizational Role Matrix: Acme Landscaping

Role	Key Questions	Responsibilities	Deliverables	Measures
John (as Organizational Leader)	What are the major threats and opportunities for our business over the next few years?	To add value: 1) Acquire new customers, *tactically* and strategically located in specific neighborhoods. 2) Recruit and retain key employees to match customer growth. 3) Manage resources to increase profit margins.	Strategic plans for fulfilling responsibilities 1 and 2. An operational plan that will yield responsibility 3.	**Outcomes:** Referrals from neighborhood associations, current, and new customers. Improved appraised values of homes we have landscaped. Reduction of loan balances and lending rates. **Increased safety for all residents.**
Cindy (as Organizational Manager)	How can I improve the profit margin and average customer satisfaction rating for work we do while doing additional work using fewer skilled employees?	To add value: 1) Ensure that all the work gets done properly. 2) Supervise work. 3) Coach workers.	Management plans that guide the work toward the goals in accordance with the policies.	**Outputs:** The costs, benefits, and deliverables associated with goods and services. **Endorsements by neighborhood associations.** (The Output measures must be aligned with the Outcome measures.)
Individual Performers	How can I do what I have to do to keep my job?	To add value: Ensure that my work is done well.	Completed work products that support management, operational, and strategic plans.	**Products:** The costs, benefits, and deliverables associated with my work.

Dale: Good point. A lot of it is out of her control. Is it under your control?

John: Under control? That's a myth! It is not under my total control and it is not under Cindy's total control.

Dale: That is exactly right and important. That is why leadership and management are a challenge. You simply cannot control key variables. It is like surfing. Master surfers do not control the waves, they just know how to ride them. Business is like that.

Cindy: Is that why you call it "responsibility?" We can't control it, but it is our responsibility to deal with it anyway?

Dale: Exactly. And that is one reason we have to talk about issues like this. The variables that are really important to Acme Landscaping require the two of you to work together. What that means is that you take on responsibility and ask for help whenever necessary.

John: I was looking at my deliverables. Those are major, all right. But I have to deliver a lot of other things, too! Like bids for jobs and speeches to the Chamber of Commerce and a ton of other things. This little box just won't hold all my deliverables!

Dale: I'll bet that is true for Cindy, too. You have to have a lot more than management plans!

Cindy: Right! Even if I have a good plan, it isn't worth any-thing unless I follow it. And to follow it, I have to deliver a lot more. Like tons of dirt and trees, all put in the right place at the right time.

Dale: I knew that! Do you want to know why I didn't write it down here?

John: I already said the box is too small!

Dale: And so is my head! Yours too, for that matter. Most successful businesspeople have a ton of information in their heads. Most of it is learned in bits and pieces and through experience. They have trouble communicating all that jumbled store of knowledge to anyone else, don't they?

Cindy: I sure did when I was trying to run a business. I wasn't as stupid as I acted, but I just couldn't get what I knew organized so I understood it, let alone communicate it to other people.

Dale: I suppose John does that perfectly.

John: Yeah. Right.

Dale: So you don't mind if we spend a little time trying to get a few things clear enough to work with so that I don't end up making a bunch of recommendations that don't work very well because of everything else.

John: I used to work for (Fortune 100 company). Consultants recommended all sorts of things that we never used. I'm not sure it can be done.

Dale: Here's a secret: It can't be done! But if the three of us work together, we can come up with some things that will do Acme Landscaping a lot of good. If we learn from one another, we can get the job done.

John: I hope so. Let's get on with it!

Dale: Okay. You see the row down at the bottom? The Individual Performers row? In addition to being on the leadership team and the management team, each of you is a key performer. Each of you has specific work products. You've already mentioned some of them. We'll capture a few of the deliverables and measures you have mentioned down there. Actually, there could be a row for each person in Acme Landscaping. I don't suppose we'll fill in a row for everybody, but it might happen sometime much later than if we organize properly.

The point here is that good direction finding requires more than collecting a lot of data. It requires organizing it in ways useful to the clients. Collaboration with clients is absolutely necessary to convert analysis data into management information. Both the analyst and the client are "learning by discovery." The wise analyst seeks strengths—in the organization and in each person—to build on. This analytic tactic has various names in the literature including "building on strengths," "catching them doing it right," "appreciative inquiry," "tact," and "good manners." Why is that wise? Because you and I and clients and other people do not listen well when being bludgeoned with things we do not understand or that impugn our competence.

TIPS FOR ANALYSIS

You can practice using the diagram just as you would practice with any tool. Strike up a conversation with a business manager or department head or process owner. Guide the conversation with questions that build on what you are hearing. Try to get information about products, customers, feedback, measures, and so on. At some point, sketch the diagram using information for that person's area of work responsibility. Then, clarify and confirm that information through further conversation. If you are surprised at how much you learn and how quickly, and the person you are talking with is actively engaged, you are doing it well!

There are more examples of how to collaborate with clients in finding direction in other chapters in this book. Chapter 2 illustrates analysis in not-for-profit organizations such as human service agencies. The analyses can also be performed in support departments tucked away in for-profit organizations. The line of sight toward value added is often blurred at the beginning of an analysis, but the line of sight toward measured value added should never be blurred when the analysis is complete.

Summary

Finding direction for performance improvement require asking the right questions, tenaciously to:

1. Get information about the context in which the effort will occur

2. Search for critical issues facing the organization and the people in it

3. Convert the data into information

4. Organize the information so that it can be linked directly to action

The analysis is guided by four standards:

1. Focus on results and help clients focus on results.

2. Look at situations systemically, taking into consideration the larger context including competing pressures, resource constraints, and anticipated change.

3. Add value in how you do the work and through the work itself.

4. Utilize partnerships or collaborate with clients and other experts as required.

The four standards are interrelated and inseparable.

The presentation of the results of an analysis should yield:

1. Shared understanding
2. Plans for further research
3. Plans for practical action

Endnotes

1. International Society for Performance Improvement (2006). *Standards of Performance Technology and Code of Ethics* (see http://www.certifiedpt.org/index.cfm?section=standards)

2. Horn, R. E. (1989). *Mapping hypertext: Analysis, linkage, and display of knowledge for the next generation of on-line text and graphics*. The Lexington Institute. (see also http://www.stanford.edu/~rhorn/a/site/ HornRecentSpchArt.html)

3. Ausubel, D. P. (1960). The use of advanced organizers in the learning and retention of meaningful verbal material. *Journal of Educational Psychology, 51*(5), 267–272.

4. Brethower, D. M. (2004). *Behavioral systems analysis: Fundamental concepts and cutting edge applications. Part III The Total Performance System.* (see http://behavior.org/performanceMgmt/ index.cfm?page=http%3A//behavior.org/performanceMgmt/brethower _BSA_Part3.cfm)

5. LaFleur, D., and Brethower, D. M. (1998). *The transformation: Business strategies for the 21st century.* Grand Rapids, MI: Impact Groupworks.

Chapter 2
The System Thinking Lens

Overview: Systemic Context

Neither you nor I can control everything that is important and necessary to improve performance. We cannot control what happens to our business associates or our clients when they leave a meeting with us and go out into the organization to encounter the booming-buzzing confusion created by all the people with differing agendas.

I really hate that because it makes my life difficult. *Some* of the variables are out of my control and always will be—whether I am focusing on my role as a human being trying to manage and improve my own performance or on my role as an executive or manager trying to manage and improve organizational perform- ance. Some of the people I would wish were helping me will be doing things that compete with what I want. Bummer! Wouldn't it be nice if life and business were rigged in your favor (and mine)?

TIPS FOR ANALYSIS

An analyst's job is to work with clients to find a set of worthy improvement goals and then a set of variables that would enable the client to achieve the goals. The analysis is complete when the goals are clear and the variables are identified in a way that guides action steps. Anything less is more likely to add cost than net value.

"That would enable the client" is the operative phrase in the tip above. The goal is to *enable the client* to do something, something that is different from what the client is now doing. The goal is not to do an elegant analysis or dazzle the client with your brilliance, charm, and command of jargon.

But here's a fact of organizational life that makes *enabling the client* a difficult task:

There is *no* set of variables that the client can control that is sufficient to achieve organizationally significant perform-ance improvement goals.

A good analyst will discover many variables that are *important and influential, yet cannot be controlled* by the client.

There are real constraints that must be monitored and respected, even though they cannot be changed. Please reflect on your experiences in organizations to understand why that is so important. Or conduct an Internet search on the terms *intercon-nectedness, systemic,* or *constraints.* Read and ponder some of the things you find.

If you wish to get other supporting evidence from close to home, you can do so by interviewing a few successful leaders. You can get additional confirming evidence by thinking about your family or by interviewing successful parents. Think about it: You can't control what happens to your loved ones when they go off to school or to work or to church or to a ball game or to a park or to a street corner or to a political rally. They will encounter people who have different values, different agendas, and different ideas. Some people will be doing things specifically designed to recruit people to a cause that is not in the best interest of your loved ones. Such people include upstanding citizens, time-share salesmen, drug pushers, and consultants as well as pedophiles, preachers, and politicians.

Knowing that the world is not designed to fulfill the clients' agendas, a competent analyst should help clients or management teams focus on two sets of variables:

1. A set of variables the client or team can control that are *necessary but not sufficient* to achieve performance goals

2. A set of variables that are out of the client's or team's control but *must be attended to anyway* or else the client or team will be in deep trouble much of the time

In other words, the analyst is looking for a set of variables that can be managed *and* a set of variables that cannot be managed. Working with the latter variables is like breathing mountain air: You can manage how rapidly you walk, but you cannot manage the oxygen content of the air. You can manage how you attempt to change performance, but you cannot manage many of the organizational variables that impact the performance.

TIPS FOR ANALYSIS

You must work within organizational constraints just as you must walk within the constraint of the oxygen content of the air. You can work with the client to change some of the constraints, but not all of them.

The variables in the out-of-our-control set are related to the threats, constraints, and opportunities that make up the context for managing performance. The out-of-our-control variables include rainfall in China, economic conditions in India, monetary policies of at least a dozen nations, the cost of energy, the cost of labor, the availability of people with essential skill sets, the wants of potential customers, the competence of competitors, the courage of investors, the capabilities of suppliers, organizational practices and policies, and who goes on vacation at just the wrong time. We can do our best to monitor the out-of-our-control variables and recognize that such variables provide the context and constraints for identifying the (relatively) controllable variables that are necessary to bring about and sustain performance improvement.

The good news is that a systemic and collaborative approach can help deal with the out-of-our-control reality and perhaps identify internal organizational constraints that could be changed. A systemic and collaborative approach can enable experts in performance improvement to add measured value.

A systemic and collaborative approach can be a major competitive edge, but only if we get very good at seeing organizations through a systemic lens.

Chapter 2 identifies a small number of very important systemic concepts involved in businesses, families, and other living systems. It illustrates some of the reasons ISPI thought leaders articulated CPT Standard #2[1]: "Look at situations systemically, taking into consideration the larger context including competing pressures, resource constraints, and anticipated change."

Fundamental Systemic Concepts

Looking at situations systemically and competently is easier when supported by knowledge of a few basic systemic properties. In addition, looking at situations systemically requires orderly ways to obtain and use systemic information. Specific applications of generic problem-solving strategies, such as ISPI Certification Standards 5 through 10, work well for that purpose. The "orderly ways" illustrated in this book can be readily grasped by performance improvement experts who have used "orderly ways" tailored to specific performance improvement interventions such as developing instructional courses or job aids.

Using the orderly ways intelligently requires many examples and a great deal of guided practice. This chapter introduces the systemic concepts and provides (only) a few examples. It is a start; the material should be used by readers to guide additional practice. (Additional concepts, examples, and guidance are provided in the chapters that follow.)

The systemic concepts are introduced below[2] by showing how they operate in a family-as-system. Why? Because the family is a system we all have experienced. That experience will help readers understand how systemic concepts work in general and in a business-as-system.

A caveat: Families, like businesses, have been changing in recent decades. The specific surface characteristics of families and businesses have changed, but their fundamental systemic nature has not changed. Surface characteristics are important to a specific family, but are important to the rest of us only as one small example of the great variety of surface characteristics that can be generated by a few systemic fundamentals. Useful views of the potential value of taking a systemic approach to families can be found in two books. One summarizes an extensive research program on language development[3]; the other, published by the United Nations University Press, shows the breathtaking scope and importance of family systems work.[4]

Families and Businesses are Systems

A family is typically a not-for-profit system; a family requires sources of income. Some families operate family businesses that are for-profit. Wealthy families might even require careful tax advice to avoid being a *defacto* for-profit investment firm. Please take note: A collection of individuals working toward goals-in-common might make up a family, a business, or a not-for-profit entity. Which it is (family or business or a not-for-profit agency) is a matter of social convention and law.

No matter what constraints are provided by social conventions and laws, systems are systems are systems. Surface features differ, but fundamental systemic properties are the same.

The owner/manager of a business operates it on the basis of knowledge, experience, and intelligent guesses. All three! Parents do the same. The business decisions often get better over time as knowledge expands, lessons are learned, and guessing becomes more intelligent. And sometimes, business decisions get worse as conditions change and thinking lags behind. It is the same with families. Viewing a business-as-system or a family-as-system can help make good decisions. And it can help performance improvement analysts identify critical issues quickly.

TIPS FOR ANALYSIS

There is a two-way knowledge transfer during the analysis. You learn about the organization; the client learns just a bit about how to see the world through a systemic lens.

I will illustrate the family-as-system using an example. The example shows a family as it was when many of us were much younger and when some of us might have been too young to notice. Some people currently consider the family I will describe to be an anachronism; others consider such families to be essential for our culture to survive. It might be quite important for a family therapist or a professional association supporting family therapists to have a position on whether this concept of family is an anachronism or an essential ingredient in the survival of our society. But it is not necessary for most of us to have a position on that matter. We can understand families-as-systems without taking a position on the issue. I mention the matter only to provide one more example of a key point: Understanding the context is important; *different contexts yield different priorities regarding key variables* even though the systemic functions do not change.

In contrast to the systemic properties, the surface properties of specific systems vary enormously. My family looks much different than it did 20 years ago. The American Association for Retired Persons is a lot different than it was 20 years ago. Microsoft today is probably much different than what Microsoft will be in 20 years. Systems change. The basic and general properties of systems do not. There are a few systemic functions performed in all families (except for those that are already falling apart because the functions are not performed).

Here is a very important notion about sameness and differences in systems:

- All families are the same;
  each family is unique.

- All businesses are the same;
  each business is unique.

- All not-for-profits are the same;
  each not-for-profit is unique.

- All individuals are the same;
  each individual is unique.

The systemic properties provide the "samenesses" that enable us to understand the "uniquenesses." Families are all the same in just the same sense that cities are all the same or flower gardens are all the same or governments are all the same. Each system is a member of a *category* (family, city, flower garden, government), but each is unique. Albany might have a few street names in common with Atlanta, but the map of each city is unique. Each is a unique city, but a city all the same.

Many details contribute to the uniquenesses; a few details contribute to the samenesses. It is the samenesses that are defining. The samenesses provide the anchors, the intellectual underpinnings, the schemata, the lenses, the perspectives that support understanding. The details provide the uniquenesses.

The systemic properties summarize the samenesses that enable the analyst to understand and capture key uniquenesses. Therein is the power of system thinking.

Your family is very different than mine, and both our families are very different from several others we could mention. But there are a few fundamental functions in common. Acme Landscaping is very different from several other landscaping businesses. But there are a few fundamental functions in common.

TIPS FOR ANALYSIS

Ask questions to get at samenesses and unique-nesses:

- How is your family similar to families you admire? Families you dislike?

- How is your business similar to the business of your main competitor? How is it different?

- What are some of the good things about people around here? Things that they have in common? Things that they agree upon? What do they disagree about?

- What are some of the things your best manager does? How does that differ from managers who are not as effective?

- What are the characteristics of some of your best customers? How does that differ from other customers?

- What are some of the best performance measures you have? What are some of the worst? What do the best have in common? How does that differ from the other measures?

The unchanging and invariant nature of systemic properties is no accident. The properties enable living systems to live in changing environments. Each system, for example, survives (or not) through value exchanges with an external environment. A business survives (or not) through value exchanges with suppliers and customers and investors and governing bodies and, thereby, local economies and communities. Furthermore, what were "national" and "international" economies and communities only a few years ago are, increasingly, "local" in terms of interactions with the business. (It helps if the analyst knows such things, does it not?)

The people developing general systems theory sought to find the basic properties in common among a great variety of very different systems. For example, they note that all biological systems take in "food" and give off "waste." Animals eat plants and other eaters-of-plants and give off a variety of waste products. Plants thrive on many of the wastes, including carbon dioxide, and give off a variety of wastes, including oxygen.

One system's waste is another system's food. What "costs" one system adds value to another. Animals thrive on the planet because plants thrive on the planet. Sellers thrive in an economic system because buyers thrive in an economic system. Absent plants, animals would not survive; absent animals, some plants would do all right, but others would not. Absent buyers, sellers would not survive; absent sellers, some (former) buyers would do all right, others would not. It is just this sort of thing that gives rise to concepts such as ecology or commerce or economics or any one of many other disciplines.

Think hard about the preceding paragraph and you might identify at least two key concepts of general systems theory. You might discover:

- Interdependence
- Value exchange

Living systems survive through value exchanges and, hence, are interdependent with many other living systems and a few non-living systems as well. The system analyst is not required to take a position on the Gaia Hypothesis, that the rocks and rivers of earth, along with the sun and moon and stars, comprise a living system.[5,6] But the analyst should be aware of the potential interdependencies among families and businesses and the earth, moon, sun, and stars.

TIPS FOR ANALYSIS

Look for interdependencies. "What makes the relationship with your best customers work? How does
the customer benefit from the relationship? How do
you benefit from that aspect of the relationship?"
"What makes the relationship with your best suppliers
work? How does the supplier benefit? How do you
benefit? What can you do to ensure that you both
continue to get value from the relationship?"

Interdependence and value exchanges are basic to societies
and economies and businesses and families. Given interdependence, where does one system stop and another start? Are the customers and the employees and investors part of the business? Yes
and no. The analyst does not have to take a position on whether
employees are part of the business, suppliers of labor, or inde-
pendent contractors. When I get a haircut, I am physically *in* the
barber's business, but I am not *part* of the business. (Or am I? If
you seek to buy the barber's business, much of the value and price
will be determined by the customer list.)

Just what are the boundaries of a business? It is not easy to
know, but the concept of a system boundary is an important systemic concept. Lawyers and governmental agencies such as the
Internal Revenue Service argue about where the system boundary
is. The system analyst should know that "system boundary" is a fundamental systemic concept—what is part of the system and what is
part of the environment?

The concept of system boundary is a very important concept.
Have you ever watched an infant struggle to learn whether "that
moving object down there" is part of "me" (what you and I call a
"foot") or part of the external world? Similarly, there is an unseen
boundary between Ford Motor Company and everything else or
between your family and everything else. Consider the boundary
that defines "our nation" or "our company" or "our neighborhood" or
"me" or "our trademark" or "our customers" or "potential customers"
or "our industry" or "our values" or....

Some value exchanges occur within system boundaries,
between family members, between divisions, between workers.
Other value exchanges occur across system boundaries when

supplies are purchased, goods are sold, dividends are paid, taxes are paid, and viruses enter humans or computers. And the value exchanges that occur within system boundaries are often quite different than those that cross system boundaries. I can say things to my wife that you had better not say! I can say things to my children that you have no business saying. If someone starts talking about "internal customers" while you are doing an analysis, worry about whether the value exchanges with "internal customers" add value to the organization and paying customers. Value exchanges between "internal customers" might be in the realm of culture, economics, or both. An analyst, whether asking questions about a business or about a family, will miss important information unless the many value exchanges are identified and understood.

TIPS FOR ANALYSIS

Questions like these can identify important information and key variables:

- How do you make your money?
- What is the best thing about working together?
- What would happen if you could not do that anymore?
- What would cause you to lose customers?
- What would cause morale to drop?
- What gives you the most satisfaction about your family?
- What are the shared goals or values in your family?
- What would cause my family members to become dysfunctional?
- What would happen if...?

Value exchanges can be material (money for goods) or informational (I'll give you $100 to tell me how to repair my furnace) or somewhere in between (I'll scratch your back if you scratch mine). The concept of value exchange has been a fundamental concept of economics since 1776 when Adam Smith published *The Wealth of Nations*, a truly great book now available online.[7] Goods are usually material and services are often informational. Information is often exchanged along with goods (this flower will thrive in wet, rich, shaded soil). Families have definite boundaries; it is (usually) easy to know whether someone is or is not a member of a family. (But is weird Aunt Sally who lived with us really a part of the family now that she has her own apartment? And what about the neighbor's child who always seems to be under foot?)

Two other concepts, learning and feedback, are also very important, especially in families and businesses. The concepts relate to these two questions: How are we doing? and How can we get better and better at what we do? (These two concepts will be featured later.)

One Family Viewed as a System

Let us consider a specific, somewhat typical, family: two adults, two children; adults 40ish, children 4 and 7. Both adults work, he too many hours, she fewer hours because she is just resuming her career and because the couple is still in the habit of letting most of the childcare responsibilities fall on her. That is just the way it is; both parents know it, neither is happy about it, but neither feels a strong sense of urgency about rebalancing the roles. (Wilma, the wife, is beginning to feel a sense of urgency, but urgency has not reached husband Wilber's awareness.) Tammy, the 4-year-old, goes to day care and will start kindergarten next year at a nearby school where Tommy, the 7-year-old, is in 2nd grade.

The family members are very good consumers, consuming enough to put large burdens on the income producers, which is why both work.

- Wilber says the children are spoiled because they have more toys now than he and his four siblings ever had.

- Wilma says Wilber bought most of the toys and should stop complaining.

- Wilber admits he might overdo it a bit buying toys for Tammy, but insists that Wilma lets Tommy get away with anything short of beating on Tammy until she shows bruises or short of pulling out the cat's fur when the cat is not shedding.

- Wilma just shrugs her shoulders and pretends to listen.

- Wilber likes to talk about how he did many chores and how Tammy and Tommy do not; Tommy, after all, is getting old enough...

- Wilma says Wilber should know that is not how people do things anymore.

- Wilber says that is why children get into so much trouble.

They've had the argument so many times that both do it on automatic pilot. Tommy has stopped listening in. Tammy still worries a little about the arguments. Wilber and Wilma worry about how they can both work and still be good parents. The worry is not helping them work or parent.

The last time Wilma and Wilber talked about the "strategic direction" of the family was just as they became engaged. They agreed that they should have two children (ideally a boy and a girl), earn lots of money, send the children to good schools, and live happily ever after. Their early and infrequent discussions of sex were of the "I like mornings," "I like evenings" variety. The discussions now are on the topic of "What should we tell Tommy and Tammy?" Neither Wilber nor Wilma has much skill in talking with the other about sex and even less in talking with the children about the topic.

Wilma (and Wilber, sometimes) opines that if their employers ran their businesses the way Wilma and Wilber run the family, both would soon be out of a job. Wilber (and Wilma, sometimes) opines that if their employers cared as much about their employees as Wilma and Wilber care about Tommy and Tammy, work would be a lot more pleasant.

It is a successful family. They make their mortgage payments, dispose of disposable income, believe that things are not great but okay, and would think about the future more if they had the energy.

```
┌─────────────────────────────────────────────┐
│                                             │
│              TIPS FOR ANALYSIS              │
├─────────────────────────────────────────────┤
```

Always try to get clear about the client's vision of success. "If this project is successful, how will everyone know?" "If we help you develop better relationships with key customers, what will that look like? What is the look and feel of a good relationship with a customer? What are some of the numbers that will tell us the relationship is better?" "If we help you change this culture, what will be different about coming to work here? How would employees notice? How would customers notice? How would investors notice?"

Systemic Features

Interdependence

The family is a system in which the members are interdependent. The family would not have a house and mortgage without the combined incomes. Wilber and Wilma would not have Tommy and Tammy without pre-parenting cooperative coital engagements. Tommy and Tammy are dependent on Wilber and Wilma for food, shelter, and guidance. Wilber and Wilma are dependent on Tommy and Tammy for income tax deductions, frustrations, and satisfactions. The shared frustrations and satisfactions are part of the Wilber-Wilma bonding.

Value Exchanges

The interdependencies are founded on value exchanges. We'll not talk about the Wilber-Wilma value exchanges related to sexual fulfillment, but there are many other value exchanges we might talk about: laughing at one another's jokes, helping one another with household tasks, sharing enjoyable experiences at work, commiserating about bad experiences, and the like. Most of these value exchanges are unnoticed and not really thought about unless something is out of balance with respect to the exchanges.

The value exchanges with the world outside the family are very important as well. The value exchange is, after all, a basic economic concept—in my view, the driving force for Adam Smith's "invisible hand" and his more down-to-earth concepts.[8]

Each family member spans the boundary in some ways, engaging in value exchanges outside the family. Wilma thinks Wilber spans the boundary too much and should spend more time at home with Tammy and Tommy. Tommy thinks that his parents keep too close an eye on what he does outside the family. Parents are a source of necessities for children. Children are a source of little things that make life worthwhile for parents. Frequent "we value active, fun-loving children, so let us play together" exchanges benefit children much more than "we value silence so shut up or I'll smack you one" exchanges. (Hart and Risley's research shows that very clearly.[9])

Boundaries

The family is a recognized entity with definite boundaries. There are documents recorded to show family membership. If Wilber or Wilma want out of the marriage, it raises a ruckus in Wilber's family and in Wilma's family and maybe in their church and at their workplaces. It might take litigation and would certainly require filing legal documentation to dissolve the marriage.

If Tommy teases Tammy a bit too much, that is almost acceptable to Wilma and Wilber and most people in the neighborhood. But it is a different story if Tommy teases the cute child down the street a bit too much. That is not as acceptable to some people: "You can't do that to MY child!" Tommy might be considered a bit naughty for within-the-boundary teasing of Tammy. He might be considered a pre-delinquent on a downward trajectory for boundary-spanning-teasing of the other child.

If asked about the purpose of the family, Tommy might say, "To keep me from having fun!" and Tammy might say, "To keep Tommy from being mean." What Wilber and Wilma say will be influenced by the mood they are in at the moment, but they might say something that they learned from their parents or in church or in civics classes. A sociologist would have one answer, an economist another. But both the sociologist and the economist would have an important answer, correct, but complete only from a narrow perspective.

Tommy learns, in the family, by getting constructive feedback from Wilma and Wilber and Tammy, though Tommy might not admit that Tammy's feedback is ever constructive. Tommy learns what others consider appropriate by their verbal statements and specific actions. He learns that heeding the advice and admonishments of his parents can keep him out of trouble and help him be successful outside of the family. (Tommy is more fortunate than a child living in a dysfunctional family.)

Some families seem to spend a lot of time happily helping one another; other families seem to be happiest when they are fighting with one another. *Each family system has its own dynamic, but each family system has a dynamic.* Actually, each family has more than one dynamic, acting one way during a crisis, another way during the week, another way on Sunday, another way when guests are present or grandmother Allison visits. Each family is unique. At the same time, each family is a system very much like other families. A similarity is in having a unique dynamic; the difference is the uniqueness of the dynamic. (Please make note of the preceding sentence; it is quite important to know about uniqueness/sameness as we analyze families or businesses or not-for-profit agencies.)

Resources are obtained by crossing system boundaries. Some parents work and some families are also family businesses. The family business is and was quite common in the case of family farms, grocery stores, restaurants, and all those businesses called "mom and pop" businesses.

The children perform much of the work in family businesses, at least at the start and at least in families called "ethnic minorities," especially those ethnic minorities that thrive within majority cultures. Obtaining and developing new employees is quite important and sometimes a lot of fun! "Mom and pop" businesses have often been supported by large families.

Families that are also family businesses differ from other families primarily in the sources of revenue (many customers vs. one or two jobs) and in the frequency of interactions among family members.

> "Why do you get along so well with your wife?" "I don't have a choice. I have to work with her all day and sleep with her all night."

> "Why do you get along so well with your children?" "I don't have a choice. If we didn't get along, I'd lose all my employees."

What is more, the systemic features for a family are the same as the systemic features of a business. That is why we refer to *general* systems theory. If you wish to find out more about some of the key concepts of general systems theory, do Internet searches on some of the key words such as: "general systems theory," "systemic," "system boundary," "interconnectedness," "value exchange," "subsystem maximization." (When typing the key words, type the quotation marks, but not the commas.)

Connecting Analysis Questions to Systemic Issues

Each business is unique, but each is a business and each is a system. The systemic features make it manageable and the uniquenesses make it profitable. Or not.

The samenesses cannot be seen by looking at what is in front of the analyst's nose. The samenesses are discovered by looking below the surface, at the function or purpose of what the analyst sees. James G. Miller makes that very clear in his magnum opus, *Living Systems.*[10]

Consider questions that a performance improvement analyst asks to find direction. These samples are copied directly from Chapter 1.

- What is the direction (the mission, the goals, the strategy) of the organization?
- What is working well?
- What should be improved?
- Why? (And why? And why? And why?)
- What is going on in the organization that will help the effort? That will hinder or compete with the effort?
- Who are the key players?
- If the project is a success, what will success look like?
- How will stakeholders (inside and outside the organization) benefit?

Here are the questions again, as they might be asked in an analysis at Acme Landscaping:

- How do you guide Acme Landscaping toward the future? What are some of the current goals and dreams?
- What is working well? What is an example of that?

- What should be improved? What is an example of that?
- Why? (And why? And why? And why?)
- What is going on in Acme Landscaping that will help the effort? That will hinder or compete with the effort?
- Who are the key players?
- If Acme is a success, what will success look like?
- How will people inside and outside Acme benefit?

Here they are again, as they might be asked in an analysis of a typical family:

- How do you guide the family toward the future? What are some of the current priorities and dreams?
- What is working well? What is an example of that?
- What should be improved? What is an example of that?
- Why? (And why? And why? And why?)
- What is going on in the family that you are proud of?
- What is going on that you do not like to see?
- How are Wilber and Wilma developing? Tammy and Tommy?
- If the family is a success, what will success look like?
- How will people inside and outside the family benefit?

TIPS FOR ANALYSIS

Please understand that these questions are opening questions and conversation starters. Notice that the fourth bullet is actually a "rolling why" question that applies at times to any and all of the other questions. The terms used in phrasing the questions are tailored to the specific system and would become more tailored as the conversation moves forward.

Please understand also that the person being interviewed will have enthusiasms and reservations. A good analyst will follow up on the enthusiasms as long as they are yielding useful information. Making the judgment about whether or not the enthusiasms are yielding useful information is a judgment that gets better with experience. In my experience, it is usually wise to respect reservations, noticing them and moving on, and maybe coming back to them later. It is usually counterproductive to act like a physician stupidly pushing on an abdomen that might contain a ruptured appendix. It is better to have a more gentle touch and come back to the area again. Sore spots are important, but deal with them when you can do so supportively, after the client has learned to trust you a bit. The client will be more likely to trust you if you demonstrate that you understand and appreciate some of the good intentions and good work.

Here are some Acme questions from Chapter 1, listed, then paraphrased for a family:

- What is Acme's market segment?
- What is their value promise to customers?
- What is Acme's competitive strategy?
- How does Acme market?
- How does the family fit into the neighborhood? Into an extended family?
- What is the image of the family that you want people to have?
- How do you help everyone understand your family's unique strengths? Understand how and why this is a good family?
- What do you do to ensure that the family has a good image? That each family member earns a good reputation?

Practice Using a Systemic Lens to Find Direction

The systemic lens not only helps the analyst frame questions to get at important issues, but it also helps the analyst organize answers to be useful in guiding action. With practice, the systemic lens fades from consciousness and becomes automatic and intuitive. The relevant research suggests that it takes a huge amount of guided practice. A wise analyst, like a wise musician, practices a lot.

TIPS FOR ANALYSIS

A good way to practice asking systemic questions is to "interview" yourself about where you work. Use questions similar to those above, paraphrasing them to fit your situation. Then "interview" yourself about your family. You might find it beneficial to script the questions before you begin each interview. Script only a half-dozen key open-ended leading questions you will ask first. Ask yourself follow-on questions based on your answers. (It works! You will probably discover things you did not know you know and discover things you do not know but wish you did.)

Self-interviews are useful exercises to get the feel of the analysis. Another, maybe better, exercise is to interview a close friend about the friend's workplace and family. Another, maybe better, exercise is to paraphrase some of the questions above in doing a retrospective analysis of a project you and your colleagues have already completed.

I will provide additional tools in later chapters, but for now, just practice with the questions above. Please get comfortable with paraphrasing the questions and asking follow-on questions now. Fluency will come with much practice. (Organizing the answers will also be dealt with in much more detail later on, especially in Chapters 3 and 4.)

Later chapters will show how to identify the critical out-of-management-control variables and the necessary-but-not-sufficient variables. Three sets of tools will be used: Brethower's Total Performance System and Mission Statement tools, Kaufman's concepts of Mega, Macro, and Micro analysis, and Rummler's Anatomy of Performance tools.[11] The tools help the analyst discover ways to bring the out-of-management-control and the necessary-but-not-sufficient variables into alignment to improve system performance. Doing so will enable the analyst to fulfill the four fundamental ISPI standards of focusing on results, taking a system view, adding value, and working collaboratively. I know of no other way (other than the way described in this book) to fulfill all four standards consistently. If there is another way, I'll find it, eventually, but I hope you find it sooner!

Summary

Both halves of these statements are true:

- All businesses are the same; each business is unique.

- All families are the same; each family is unique.

- Families and businesses are just the same; families are really very different than businesses.

Both the samenesses and the uniquenesses are extremely important to those of us who seek to improve the performance of businesses. The samenesses are in systemic features: features all systems have in common—the "deep structure" of the systems. The uniquenesses are in the surface features, in the things that differentiate you from me and your business from my business.

Interdependence, value exchange, and system boundary are very important systemic concepts. Value exchanges provide mutual benefits and sustain the interdependent relationship. Some value exchanges such as the exchange of money for goods occur across system boundaries. Some value exchanges such as the exchange of information occur within system boundaries.

The analyst seeks to help the client find a set of variables that the client can manage in order to improve performance. Yet, there are always some variables the client cannot control, but that make up the set of constraints within which the client must work.

Endnotes

1.   International Society for Performance Improvement (2006). *Standards of Performance Technology and Code of Ethics* (see http://www. certifiedpt.org/index.cfm?section=standards)

2. Internet searches. Key words: "general systems theory," "systemic," "system boundary," "interconnectedness," "value exchange," "subsystem maximization" (use quotes, but not commas).

3. Hart, B., & Risley, T. (1995). *Meaningful differences in the everyday experiences of young children.* Baltimore, MD: Brookes Publishing.

4. Zeitlin, M. F., Megawangi, R., Kramer, E. M., Colletta, N. D., Babatunde, E. D., & Garman, D. (1995). *Strengthening the family: Implications for international development.* New York: United Nations University Press. (see: http://www.unu.edu/unupress/unupbooks/ uu13se/uu13se00.htm)

5. Chamberlin, S. (2005). Dr. C's remarkable ocean world. (see http:// www.oceansonline.com/gaiaho.htm)

6. Lovelock, J. E. (1979). *Gaia: A new look at life on Earth.* Oxford University Press.

7. Smith, A. (1776). *An inquiry into the nature and causes of the wealth of nations.* Edinburg, Scotland. Online edition © 1995-2005 Adam Smith Institute. (see http://www.adamsmith.org/smith/won/won-index. html)

8. See note 7 above.

9. See note 3 above.

10. Miller, J. G. (1978). *Living systems.* New York: McGraw-Hill.

11. See the first book in this series by Roger Kaufman, *Change, choices, and consequences: A guide to Mega thinking and planning* (Amherst, MA: HRD Press. 2006); see also Appendix A.

Chapter 3
Systems Analysis of a Business

Overview: The Systemic Perspective

We seek not to *change* performance but to *improve* performance. You can change your investment tactics and strategies much more easily than you can change your investment performance. You can help supervisors change the way they interact with team members much more easily than you can help them improve the team's work performance. The difference between *performance change* and *performance improvement* is quite large and quite important. That came as a huge surprise to me. I imagined that any request for change would be a wise request that would point directly to an intervention that would yield an improvement. After all, the requestors work in the organization and know the relevant operations much better than I. Unfortunately, people who request interventions are no more omniscient than you or I. Each of us knows a lot and none of us knows everything.

When I began work in our field more than 40 years ago, I knew precious little about *improving* performance. I knew a lot about *changing* performance (I say, defensively), but I simply did not understand the Bhuddist story of the Blind Men and the Elephant.[1] I just thought those blind men were foolish. "Imagine grabbing hold of an elephant's tail or tusk or leg or ear or trunk or banging into his big belly and thinking that you knew what the whole elephant was like!" I thought, feeling quite superior. "An elephant is *not* 'very like a rope' or 'a tusk' or 'a tree' or 'a snake' or 'a fan' or 'a wall'; those are just features of parts of the elephant! Each might be an important part, but it is *only a part* of the elephant!"

Little did I realize that my thinking demonstrated a thorough misunderstanding of the moral of the story. The moral was not "Some people are foolish!" but "Everyone's knowledge is limited." It might be true that some people are foolish, but the important moral to learn is that *any human being operates on limited and incomplete knowledge.* (This is part of the rationale for ISPI's collaboration standard.)

TIPS FOR ANALYSIS

Here is the first thing to know about (almost) any request for an intervention:

The request is like a request to tie a rope to an elephant's tail!

Accepting a request at face value can help you build a temporary relationship with a client by doing an intervention that changes performance. Improving performance is another matter; changing performance might make performance worse and reduce your credibility.

A request might be well-intentioned, but please do not stake your reputation on the assumption that the request is well-informed. It is unwise to blindly accept a request—or to spurn it. It is far better to know a lot about any organization in which performance improvement is desired. You might be able to help the client in a way that would delight the client if the client knew it could be done! One way of knowing a lot about an organization is to know some of the organization's systemic properties. To improve an elephant's tail, you must know how the tail adds value to the elephant. The systemic properties enable you to quickly learn how the part (the tail) adds value to the whole (the elephant). The systemic properties help you discover how the elephant adds value to his owner/manager and the owner/manager's customers and the community and maybe even to you or your neighbor next door. The systemic properties make up the intellectual scaffolding that supports the detailed work of performance improvement.

A Lens for Viewing the World out There

An organization, any organization, operates in three worlds. Roger Kaufman, in another volume in this series, and elsewhere,[2] has described the three worlds: Mega, Macro, and Micro. The Mega World is the whole enchilada—the world at large. It is the global community and the ecosystems and the economic systems and the cultures. The influences of the Mega World on the organization may seem as slight as the gentle waves of the ocean in front of a beach house. But the influences of the Mega World can be huge and inexorable, like the waves of the ocean pounding a beach house to smithereens during a Category 4 hurricane.

The owner of a beach house might enjoy the beach today, not thinking much about hurricane forces. The builder of the house should have thought about that! And the owner of the house should consider the power of hurricanes while making repairs or mooring a boat. Similarly, a farmer in Kansas might have been free to ignore much of the wide world years ago, but today's farmer is likely to have an uplink that provides access to data about rainfall in Russia and political developments in countries that provide markets for Kansas farm crops. And the farmer in Kansas is likely to be aware that, given political and cultural unrest half way around the world, a son or daughter might go off to risk life and limb to protect the freedom to farm. Families, businesses, and not-for-profit agencies exist in the Mega World even if people in them (for a time) successfully ignore the Mega World. Some Mega World information is vital to understanding a system and doing systemic analyses.

An organization, any organization, operates within the Mega World and it also operates in the Macro World. The Macro World is the world of commerce—the world of products and services and suppliers and customers and competitors and strategic allies. It is the business world; the agency's area of service; the family's friends and neighbors. Is it important for a performance improvement analyst to learn about that Macro World? Of course! It almost goes without saying—but too often goes without being done competently.

A person in any organization also operates in the Micro World. The Micro World is the world of the workplace, including the work and workers and widgets and interpersonal relationships and friendships and rivalries and organizational cultures. It is the world that employees all know and sense and feel and touch and experience.

Some people inside an organization can be so enmeshed in the Micro World that they are totally oblivious to the fact that there is a Mega World out there. (A wise analyst will check to be sure that "some people" are not the leaders and executives.) Some people inside an organization can be almost oblivious to the fact that there is a Macro World, a world of exchanges of goods and services and money, a world of the exchanges that keep the organization in existence and out of bankruptcy. But no one in an organization is oblivious to the Micro World, the world of co-workers and managers and confusion and fellowship and conflict and intrigue, a world in which "we" are okay and "they" are not. Unless your client is a very senior executive, perhaps the chief executive officer (but probably not the chief operating officer), the Micro World is what the client experiences most vividly.

Not very long ago, most business courses and many managers could focus on the Micro World and be current—not wise, but it was common. The Macro World might have been the focus of a course or two in marketing and a course or two in finance, but that was about the extent of it. And the Mega World was left to dreamers and thinkers and people who felt no sense of urgency about getting anything whatsoever of a practical nature accomplished!

What do Mega and Macro and Micro have to do with improving the performance of widget makers, builders of mother boards, counters of beans, and shoe-ers of draft horses? Anyone seeking to improve performance has a challenge. They cannot just change performance as if rearranging the deck chairs on the *Titanic*. They must look, both closely and in a far-seeing way, at the consequences of the performance they seek to improve.

Some people in the organization must be attuned to all three: the Mega, the Macro, and the Micro Worlds. A primary cause of the performance problem is likely to be a short-sighted focus on the Micro World. Indeed, one of the greatest challenges for the systems analyst and the would-be performance improver is to find ways to align the actions of people with the surging seas of the Mega and Macro Worlds. That, incidentally, was why my colleagues and I created the Total Performance System diagram many years ago. The diagram represents the Micro view with a rectangle labeled "Processing System," that is, the part of the system that does the work. The "Receiving System" box in the Total Performance System diagram is the part that receives the goods or services of the Processing System. The Receiving System represents the Macro and the Mega views. (The Total Performance System diagram shown later in Figure 3.2 uses "Acme" to label the Processing System and "The World Acme Interacts With" to label the Receiving System.)

When we seek to improve performance (not merely change it), we seek to align Mega and Macro and Micro variables through specific actions of specific people. Teamwork is involved. Collaboration is involved. So too is the entire organizational infrastructure. All that infrastructure, including the parts operated by engineers, accountants, human resource people, and techies at all levels, must be aligned for performance improvements to *be* improvements and to be lasting improvements.

That is the challenge of the systemic view—seeing all parts of an issue and getting all the little parts to work together to form a coherent big picture. A project that focuses only on improving performance of process X or in Department Y is not meeting the challenge. In fact, and in accord with the subsystem maximization principle, improving one little system is quite likely to make the total system worse!

No project can bring about complete alignment, but every performance improvement project should be a step in that direction. Finding direction and getting everyone to work together to go there is fundamental to what we do if we actually work in accord with the four ISPI Standards[3]:

1. Focus on results! *Which results?*

2. Systemic results that align the parts of the organization and add value! *Add value to whom?*

3. Value to specific stakeholders (without subtracting value from others)! *Add value, how?*

4. Collaboratively! *Why? Because no one person has as many hands and heads and hearts as it takes to do it all!*

Did I neglect to tell you that this work is not easy? It is easy to understand, once you understand a few fundamentals, just as the theory of weight loss is easy to understand but difficult to do. Applying the theory takes diligent and intelligent action. That might be why some people despise theory.

A Systemic Perspective: The Anatomy of Performance

I have an anatomy. So too does my performance and your performance and the performance of Acme Landscaping. Let us look first at the anatomy of performance for Acme. Geary Rummler, in common with many analyzers of performance, works in pictures and diagrams and stories. (Yes, and in words, too, but the words are subordinate to the pictures and diagrams and stories. Just as teachers of art and grammar and rhetoric have tried to tell all of us for years.) A picture of Acme Landscaping as shown in Rummler's Anatomy of Performance diagram[4] is in Figure 3.1.

Figure 3.1: Anatomy of Performance Diagram

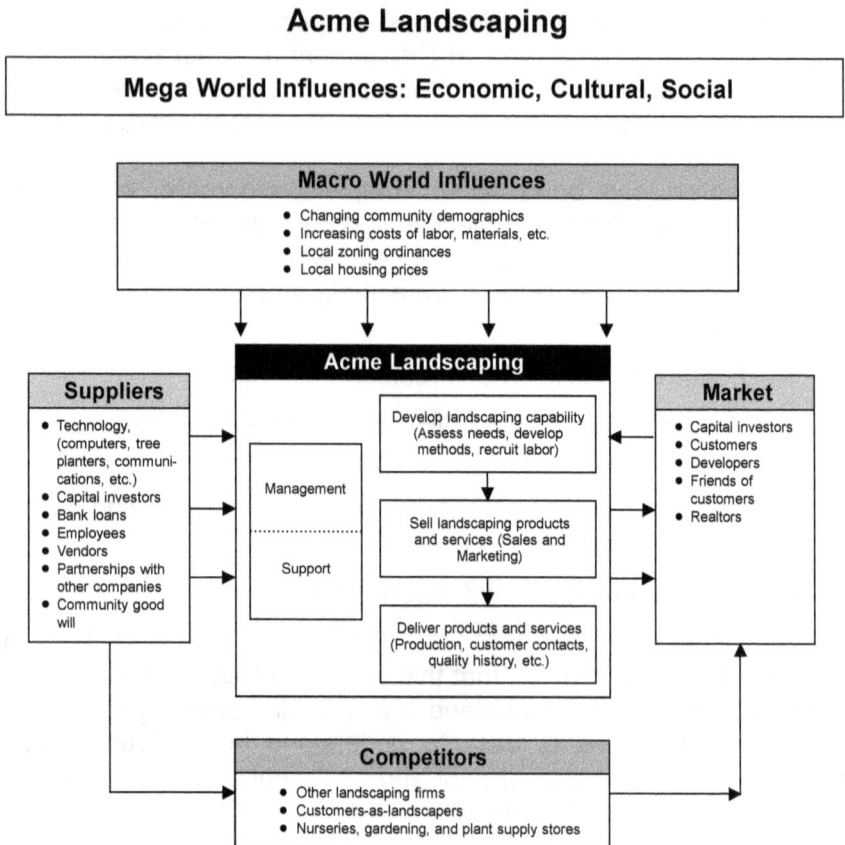

Acme Landscaping

Mega World Influences: Economic, Cultural, Social

Macro World Influences
- Changing community demographics
- Increasing costs of labor, materials, etc.
- Local zoning ordinances
- Local housing prices

Acme Landscaping

Suppliers
- Technology, (computers, tree planters, communications, etc.)
- Capital investors
- Bank loans
- Employees
- Vendors
- Partnerships with other companies
- Community good will

Management

Support

Develop landscaping capability (Assess needs, develop methods, recruit labor)

Sell landscaping products and services (Sales and Marketing)

Deliver products and services (Production, customer contacts, quality history, etc.)

Market
- Capital investors
- Customers
- Developers
- Friends of customers
- Realtors

Competitors
- Other landscaping firms
- Customers-as-landscapers
- Nurseries, gardening, and plant supply stores

Notice that the Anatomy of Performance shows the Macro World view of Acme. It focuses on the business as it is (or should be) now. There are suppliers and customers and competitors and investors that just *surround* Acme. John, owner/manager of Acme, sometimes feels surrounded and hemmed in and powerless to deal with *all* those influences on Acme's performance: Acme's performance in terms of value exchanges with customers and suppliers and investors and in comparison with competitors' and with industry averages and with what the local Chamber of Commerce and taxing authorities would like to see. The Anatomy of Performance view shows many of the out-of-our-control variables that define the potential strategic challenges and opportunities for Acme. The Anatomy of Performance view helps answer the question "Which results?" It shows the external influences and relationships that define desirable results. A one-time result that benefits only Acme might be worthy, on occasion, but not as regular fare. Sustainable, beneficial results are not zero-sum (I win/you lose), but win-win—mutually beneficial. Whom should Acme have beneficial relationships with? Customers in the marketplace, suppliers, and competitors. Why competitors? Because one day, they might merge with Acme, or go out of business and recommend Acme to their customers, or form a strategic alliance with Acme, or do something constructive with respect to the landscaping industry. Why good relationships with the Macro World influences—and sources of information about them? To identify strategic opportunities and threats, and avoid getting thrown in jail or fined or publicly castigated for something Acme does. Why good relationships with Mega World representatives, whether John and Cindy know the people or not? To identify opportunities and threats, and sleep well at night, and to achieve a sense of personal satisfaction about doing good while doing well.

How are you getting along with your suppliers, John?

"Decently. Some of them are raising prices, others are not; some are late with deliveries; others are not. My banker is happy at the moment, but my accountant is worrying and I do not know what will happen to Acme if the zoning boards and homeowners' associations keep changing their rules all the time."

How are you getting along with your customers, John?

"Really well. Cindy is doing a fabulous job! Oh, I have a couple of regular customers who complain vociferously all the time about everything, but they've been doing that for years and no other landscaper wants their business. I'm worried, though, that we aren't getting as many referrals as we want. And some of our best customers have raised their children and are tired of taking care of a big yard. Maybe I can help them get ready to sell and move into a smaller home. And maybe the new owners will become customers. But maybe not."

What are the most serious challenges you face, John?

"Prices of everything I buy are going up, just as the competition is cutting prices to steal my customers! I am getting squeezed. That's why I keep telling Cindy to watch the profit margins on each job. Right now most of the new home building is not in our market niche. It is in starter homes. The people who buy them have really tight budgets, especially because they tend to buy more house than they can afford. And the work ethic of people we can hire nowadays is about as abysmal as their skill levels! Yes. There are plenty of challenges to keep me awake at night!"

Even if John could not articulate the strategic challenges readily, the Anatomy of Performance diagram would guide the analyst toward a comprehensive set of questions that would uncover the critical business issues Acme faces now. What's more, John would recognize the questions as important to the business. In fact, the Anatomy of Performance can uncover too many issues for John or any mere mortal to grasp clearly. The analyst can help sort and prioritize the issues by using the Performance System perspective.

Another Systemic Perspective:
The Total Performance System (TPS)[5]

The mission statement in the TPS diagram in Figure 3.2 is one you have seen before. Now, however, would be a good time to notice something new about it. The terms of the mission statement connect to the marketplace and customers. Please understand, too, that "The World Acme Interacts With" includes the Macro World and the Mega World. (I do not point that out to clients, initially, unless they are inclined toward philosophical discussions. I use the diagram to summarize data/information from the client, not to confuse them with all sorts of observations that I find fascinating.)

The words "that add attractiveness to fine homes" connect to customers and the value added to customers. The words "enhancing the beauty and the economy" hint at the value added to others in addition to customers. Please understand also that "neighborhood" means not only the local neighborhood but, in keeping with the current reality, it means the global neighborhood—Mega.

Figure 3.2: TPS Diagram

Acme Landscaping

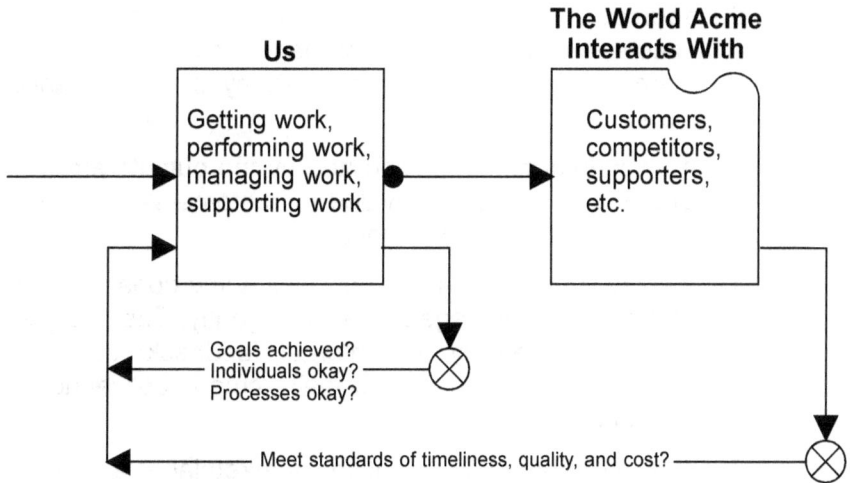

Goal Statement: Acme Home Landscaping provides landscaping services to builders and buyers that add attractiveness to fine homes, thereby enhancing the beauty and the economy of the neighborhood.

Here is an important caveat: The Acme mission statement could decay into nothing but meaningless words, as so many mission statements tend to do. John, however, with or without the help of a performance improvement analyst, can prevent that from happening.

How? I only know of one way: by attaching measures to the ideas in the Acme mission statement. Some of the measures John might consider are already shown in Figure 3.2. Notice that there are measures related to customer satisfaction, operating costs, quality, and income. Additional measures showing trends in satisfaction and income, broken down into categories of customers and including measures of increases or decreases in number of customers, bring in additional strategic measures.

I use the TPS as a summary for two basic reasons. One is that the diagram depicts the *minimum* set of measures necessary for intelligent performance.

- There are inputs. They aren't labeled in the diagram, but please understand that the input arrow symbolizes information about inputs. Take away information about inputs— the sources of plants and employees and tools and capital and cash—and John cannot manage Acme intelligently. (The inputs are labeled in the Anatomy of Performance diagram.)

- Take away information symbolized by the outputs arrow— the goods and services provided to customers—and John cannot manage Acme intelligently.

- Take away information about how well Acme does its work, and John cannot manage Acme intelligently. The information is symbolized by the internal feedback loop and includes information about how well Acme is delivering on time, on budget, and at quality.

- Take away information about the marketplace, and John cannot manage Acme intelligently. The information is symbolized by the external feedback loop about how quickly customers are paying, how satisfied they are, what they tell others about Acme, and marketplace trends.

- Take away information about Acme's mission, and John cannot prioritize all that information and manage intelligently.

The second reason for using the TPS diagram is that it has seven parts: two arrows, two boxes, two feedback loops, and the mission statement. Seven, as George Miller[6] showed many years ago, is the "magic number" that John and other mortals can keep in memory at one time. In other words, limiting the categories of information to the seven shown by the diagram makes it possible for executives and other workers to "get their head around" the information required to manage intelligently.

The diagram is sometimes called the adaptive system diagram to call attention to the fact that it captures just enough information for a system to function adaptively. By "adaptively" I mean that it can adapt to small changes in the environment by changing tactics and that it can adapt to large changes (or newly discovered opportunities) by changing goals and strategies. Absent the ability to work toward a specific set of goals (or specific and valued condition), the business or family or person could not perform well toward current goals. Absent the ability to modify goals (or direction or the condition valued), the business or family or person could not remain "in tune" with a changing environment.

A strength of the diagram is that it has few enough "parts" so that people can keep them all in focus. A weakness of the diagram is that it is too simple to show important detail. The difficulty is that the world is bigger than the inside of the analyst's and manager's heads. A mere mortal must "reduce" the vast amount of data out there into an amount of information that can be brought in through the senses and kept in active memory.

TIPS FOR ANALYSIS

The Total Performance System diagram and the Anatomy of Performance diagram are tools for organizing the data so that it can be comprehended. The Total Performance System diagram shows the forest; the Anatomy of Performance shows some of the trees and rivers running through the forest. If you look closely, you can see the Total Performance System diagram (minus the mission statement) within the Anatomy of Performance diagram.

The external complexity is real. That is why the Total Performance System (TPS) diagram can be "exploded" to show more detail. The Anatomy of Performance (AOP) diagram "explodes" the Receiving System box to show more detail. Imagine all the outer parts of the AOP exploding out of the "World Acme Interacts With" box, and you will understand the relationship between the TPS diagram and the AOP.

Another way of thinking about the relationship is that a version of the TPS diagram sits in the middle of the AOP. I'm telling you about that now just so that you know both tools link to one complex reality. The tools help us organize complex reality into simple pictures so that the analyst and the client can understand, discuss, verify accuracy, and focus action. It takes practice with these tools—the TPS and AOP—to understand them well, but they can be used with passable competence almost immediately.

Another Systemic Perspective:
The Value-Adding Processes

Neither John nor Cindy has drawn a picture that shows the work flow for Acme Landscaping. John believes he understands the work thoroughly and that Cindy understands it only moderately well. He is right. Cindy believes she understands the work thoroughly and that John understands it only moderately well. She is right.

How can both be right? Easy. John understands exactly how it was done when he was in charge of the landscaping work. Cindy understands exactly how it is done now that she is in charge. But an analyst trying to document work flow to find ways of improving it will get different stories from John and Cindy.

TIPS FOR ANALYSIS

A clever analyst would document both ways of doing the work and compare the two work flows, probably in collaboration with John and Cindy. The analyst would challenge them to figure out at least one way of doing it that is better than either of the "old" ways. Clients can usually see how to improve the process, find that exciting, and set about improving the existing process in light of the new best way.

Another Systemic Perspective:
The Support Processes

Neither John nor Cindy is an expert in bookkeeping, recruiting, hiring, compensation, truck maintenance, marketing, sales, employee relations, customer relations, supplier relations, bill collection, or any one of many other activities that must be performed to keep Acme working well.

In fact, John does some of these support processes incompetently. Some that John does incompetently, Cindy does well. Some they both do well. Some neither does well. That's the way it is in Acme and in many small businesses.

Large businesses have the same difficulties, but on a larger scale. Large businesses cope by hiring experts in X who are truly experts in X, but who aren't even close to being experts in making products and delivering services that add value to customers. Hence, the expert in X comes into conflict with the expert in Y. Typically, a human resources person who is expert in neither or not expert in business is tasked with dealing with the conflict. The conflict might be cast as a "personality conflict" or a "turf war" or "ambitious people running amuck" or some other label. Given that view, the systemic causes of the problem will rarely be found and will ensure that the problem, even if temporarily reduced, will remain.

Before accepting any "diagnosis," a performance analyst will (guess what?) analyze. Part of the analysis will be specifying a "should." What should be happening to support the value-adding processes of the business? (I do not mean "People should stop bickering!" although that might be true in many organizations.) This is the question: What value does the support process add to the business? The analyst knows that there are two (and only two) answers: The support process might reduce net cost, and/or improve the quality and timeliness of goods or services delivered.

Analysis goes much better when the analyst knows what to look for. The analyst could help John and Cindy by drawing a flowchart of the process now as a stimulus for creating a flowchart of the process as it should be. Then the analyst could figure out what it takes to make the changes to improve the processes. In short, define how the work should flow, then set out to get it to flow that way. (Yes, if the expert in X has been bickering with the expert in Y, get them together to devise the ideal work flow. Do clever interpersonal interventions or heavy-handed human resource interventions if absolutely necessary to get them to play nicely together on the task.)

Another Systemic Perspective: The Performers

The Total Performance System (TPS) diagram can be used to show the minimum conditions necessary for intelligent organizational performance. The TPS can also be used to show the minimum conditions necessary for a person to function intelligently in the organization.

Just as the TPS can be "exploded" into Rummler's AOP, it can also be exploded into Rummler's Human Performance System (HPS). I personally use the TPS as a summary for total organizations and for individuals. But sometimes I want to avoid "How can the same silly diagram be used to describe a big organization and one little worker?" In that case, I use the diagram when focusing on the individual.

Figure 3.3 shows a generic copy of the Human Performance System (HPS).[7]

Figure 3.3: Human Performance System Diagram

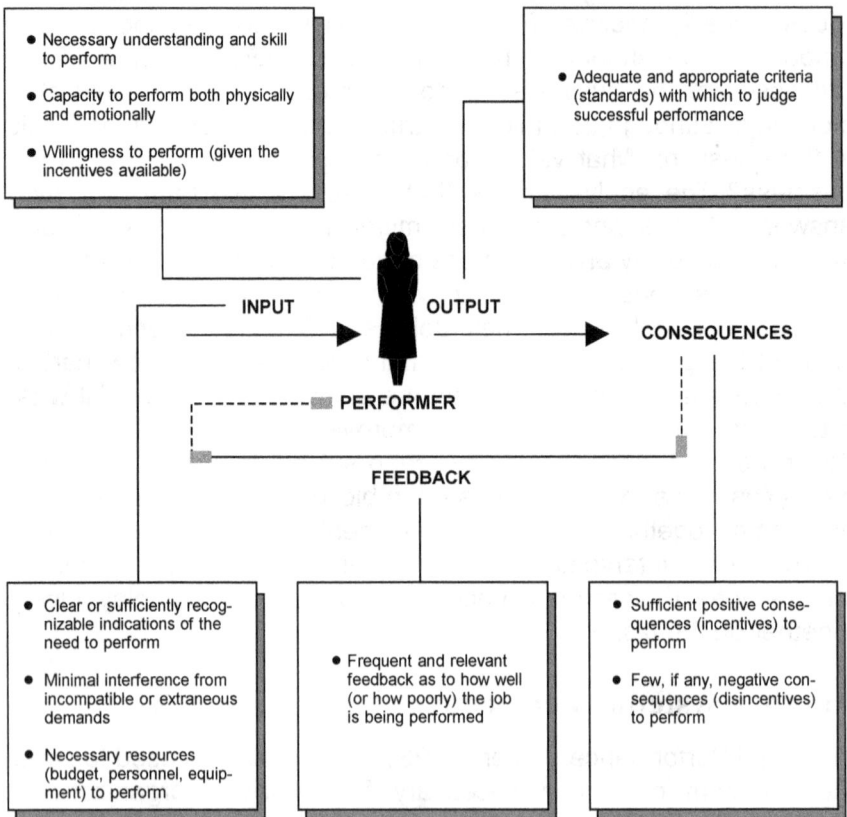

- Necessary understanding and skill to perform

- Capacity to perform both physically and emotionally

- Willingness to perform (given the incentives available)

- Adequate and appropriate criteria (standards) with which to judge successful performance

INPUT   OUTPUT   CONSEQUENCES

PERFORMER

FEEDBACK

- Clear or sufficiently recognizable indications of the need to perform

- Minimal interference from incompatible or extraneous demands

- Necessary resources (budget, personnel, equipment) to perform

- Frequent and relevant feedback as to how well (or how poorly) the job is being performed

- Sufficient positive consequences (incentives) to perform

- Few, if any, negative consequences (disincentives) to perform

Were we working with Cindy (or anyone else) to clarify the job, we would convert the generic material into specifics. For example, we would first convert the generic Output to a specific major output. For Cindy, it might be "Projects completed for customers." Then the "Adequate and appropriate criteria" would be specified: "How many projects, when, how well, and for whom?"

TIPS FOR ANALYSIS

You might want to play with the HPS diagram a little bit. Perhaps, from what you know about Cindy's work and background, you could fill in the box about Cindy's knowledge and skill, capacity, and willingness. Or you might want to fill in the HPS for yourself or a client. After doing so, you might cover up one of the parts of the HPS and ask yourself, "What would happen to the person's performance if this were weak or missing?"

I sometimes do that as a group exercise, asking subgroups to ask "What would happen if that part of the HPS were weak?" and then make the best case they can, with specific examples, that performance would soon deteriorate. I do a similar exercise with the Total Performance System and Gilbert's Behavior Engineering Model[8]; the HPS, the TPS, and the BEM are in essence alternative views of the same territory when applied at the job level. The purpose of the exercise is help people understand why all parts of the HPS, TPS, or BEM are important if good performance is to be supported.

Another Systemic Perspective:
The Management Processes

I know a small business owner who complains, much like Cindy or John would:

> "I can do every single thing that has to be done to run this business—and do it rather well! How do I know? Because I've done it! I've done it when we started, I've done it to cover for people who are on vacation, and I've done it to

cover for someone who just can't get to work that day. I can do *anything*! But that isn't enough! What has to be done is *everything*! I can't do it all myself. I have to lead and motivate and threaten and manage and all that to make sure everything gets done! And it is killing me! There must be an easier way."

There is an easier way. People talk about it in management courses and can tell you what that easier way is. It is easier if you have a good management system! Everyone knows that, right?

But what is a good management system? A performance analyst who knows the answer to that question knows something very important, does she not? A manager who does not know the answer to that question has a serious knowledge deficiency, does he not?

TIPS FOR ANALYSIS

A performance systems analyst should ask each manager, "What are the best things about the management procedures people around here use? What are some of the weaknesses? What, in your personal view, would an ideal management system be like?"

Do you know why it is important for the analyst to do that? Simple. Because if there is a deficiency in the management system, there will be deficiencies in performance. Count on it. Deming was right. Quality failures are caused by management failures.[9] Period. End of story. Yes, there are little causes, things that some people refer to as "proximate causes"—things like the tooling getting bad or the schedule being bad or people failing to get the right information from the customer. But what causes that? Management failures. What is the management team responsible for? Everything! At least that is what my boss told me once when I asked what I was responsible for as a newly anointed manager: Everything!

There are two types of management failures. I mentioned them earlier:

1. One type is the type that is "out there" and due to interactions among weather and economics and state-of-the-art and international political developments and so on—the Mega World and Macro World interactions that management must know about and adjust to.

2. The other is the type that is "in here" (almost) under our control—the Micro World things that good managers and good performers can make happen.

TIPS FOR ANALYSIS

The task of leadership is to know about the "out there" variables and devise goals and strategies for thriving in a sometimes hostile and always changing world. The task of management is to make the adjustments possible and then to make sure that the things "in here" that are (almost) controllable actually happen. To make them happen, managers must make sure that everyone has the tools and feedback and incentives and goals and such that the Human Performance System for each person says the person should have.

Providing everyone with all the ingredients of the Human Performance System is both important and challenging. That is why many of us began our careers right there, showing individual managers how to provide what was necessary for individual performers to get their work done on time, on budget, and at quality. We could do it for anyone, but the organizational requirement is to do it for everyone.

An organization must have an effective performance planning and management system if the organization is to provide the support necessary for (almost) everyone to perform well. The performance planning and management system is, if not the brain, at least the nervous system of an intelligent organization.

Summary

A person or an organization does things—performs. When we change what a person or an organization does, we are likely to make the performance a little or a lot better, a little or a lot worse, or leave performance much as it was. To make performance better, we must look beyond the person or the organization. Why? Because value does not come from "the cost of doing"—value comes from the "value of doing." If we seek to improve, to add net value, we must look beyond the performance per se. Some of us believe, with Kaufman, that we should look out not only into the Macro World, but also further out into the Mega World.

We must aid our vision with tools and technology if we are to see the Macro and Mega Worlds with reasonable clarity. The tools are necessary to bridge gaps in space and time and in the very limited knowledge each of us has.

Kaufman describes strategic planning tools that help us see clearly and beyond the end of our noses in another volume of this series and elsewhere. Rummler's Anatomy of Performance diagram helps us see clearly by specifying, in detail, how an organization relates to the Macro World. The Anatomy of Performance tool can be used to show specific links to the Mega World as well. The Total Performance System diagram and the Human Performance System diagram help to see how each person in an organization relates to the rest of the organization and to the marketplace. Furthermore, the tools work equally well for families as systems, persons as systems, businesses as systems, and not-for-profit organizaitons as systems.

Systems have specific subsystems for adding value and other subsystems that support the value-adding subsystems. A Purchasing Department, all by itself, does not add value to customers. But it can support the production subsystems so that they can add value at lower cost. Similarly, I must eat to live (my stomach is part of my internal support system). But I do not really live to eat; eating is a necessary and costly activity, but it is not my reason for being; my stomach is not a personification of who I am. Similarly, the Accounting Department or the Marketing Department or the Production Department is not a personification of the organization.

The work of complex systems such as businesses and governmental agencies is done by people—people whose work must be guided or managed or supported in order to focus efforts productively. That is true of you and me as well: We must muddle through ineptly or else our work must be guided in some way, perhaps by managers and perhaps by our own efforts at self-management. The tasks involved in performance improvement are, necessarily, interconnected and can become quite complex. That is the reason the tools of human performance improvement were invented.

Endnotes

1. An Internet search for "Blind Men" yields many items, probably including this one: http://www.cs.princeton.edu/~rywang/berkeley/258/parable.html

2. Kaufman, R. (2000). *Mega planning: Practical tools for organizational success.* Thousand Oaks, CA: Sage Publishing.

3. International Society for Performance Improvement (2006). *Standards of performance technology and code of ethics* (see http://www.certifiedpt.org/index.cfm?section=standards)

4. Additional examples of Anatomy of Performance diagrams can be found in Rummler, G. A. (2004). *Serious performance consulting: According to Rummler.* Silver Springs, MD: International Society for Performance Improvement. Additional examples can be found in Rummler, G. A., & Morrill, K. (March 2004). Know your client's business. *Performance Improvement.*

5. LaFleur, D., & Brethower, D. M. (1998). *The transformation: Business strategies for the 21st century.* Grand Rapids, MI: Impact Groupworks.

6. Miller, G. A. (1956). The magic number seven plus or minus two. *Psychological Review, 63,* 84–97.

7. Rummler, G. A., & Brache, A. P. (1995). *Improving performance: How to manage the white space on the organization chart* (2nd Ed.) San Francisco, CA: Jossey-Bass.

8. Gilbert, T. (1996). Human competencie: *Engineering worthy performance.* Amherst, MA, & Washington, D.C.: HRD Press, Inc., & The International Society for Performance Improvement.

9. Deming, W. E. (2000). *Out of the crisis.* Cambridge, MA: MIT Press.

Chapter 4
Systems Analysis of a Family

Overview: The Systemic Perspective

If we are to improve a specific behavior or performance of an organization or a person, we should understand the function of the behavior: What "good" does it do? (Or what "bad" does it do?)

- Does close supervision help or hinder performance?
- Does setting multiple goals help or hinder performance?
- Does converting to a new software program help or hinder performance?
- Does training in safety improve performance or fail to improve safety performance?

The answer to all these questions, by the way, is "Yes!"

Each can help or hinder according to the conditions already present. The performance analyst seeks to know, in advance, whether an intervention will help or hinder.

A few thousand of my colleagues[1] call that "doing a functional analysis." What are all (or nearly all) the consequences of the behavior?

- Is an executive's habit of withholding information and undercutting other executives necessary for personal survival in the organizational culture as it is now?

- Is a marketing manager's tendency to ask for a huge budget to fund a questionable campaign necessary if he is to get the small budget necessary for a vital campaign?

- Is Tommy's tendency to tease Tammy supported by the bribes he gets to be nice to Tammy?

What is the function of the behavior? And since performance results require costly behavior to attain, what is the function of specific performances in a business or agency? Do they help or hinder? (They almost always do both.)

A performance analyst must look at performance both closely and broadly in order to identify the consequences. The performance must be looked at really closely to identify the consequences to the performer. It must be looked at through a wider lens to identify the consequences to the business or agency or family or customers or neighbors or other divisions of the company or competitors or investors or other stakeholders.

What do I mean by "closely" and "broadly"? By closely I mean *really* closely—the time frame of the analysis is measured in seconds or minutes and, maybe, hours or even days. By broadly I mean *really* broadly—the time frame of the analysis is measured not only in hours or days, but in weeks and months and accounting periods and annual goals and three-year plans and farther into the future than you or I can see clearly.

Based on my 40 years or so of experience in doing analyses and watching others do them, I have to say that many analysts do not look closely enough. (The exceptions tend to be people who belong to the Organizational Behavior Management Network.) And many analysts do not look broadly enough or long enough at the total system within which the performance occurs.

TIPS FOR ANALYSIS

An analyst must have good tools and techniques and concepts in mind to find the actual (not merely intended) functions of behavior/performance. This chapter emphasizes a broad, systemic view. But please notice that the examples include a close look as well as a broad look at a system.

The systemic perspective for a family that is shown in this chapter has much in common with a systemic perspective for a business or a not-for-profit agency. The systemic features of a family, a business, and a government agency are very similar, but appear very different on the surface. Please accept the notion of systemic similarity for the moment, either heuristically to see if I support it well later on or actually because you already know it to be true. This chapter, rather than merely telling you about the fundamental similarities, will show fundamental similarities. The similarities are in what some people call the "deep structure" while the uniquenesses are in the "surface structures." This chapter will help you understand what it means to look both closely and broadly at the function of specific performances. The understanding will help you become an increasingly competent performance analyst. I promise. Please hang in there. And thank you for your effort!

A perspective, as you know, is a way that you and I and other mere mortals look at things. We each have our own perspective, built up from our experiences. We change perspectives the way we change our shoes: we try them on for a bit and then walk miles in them before we are comfortable with them. This chapter is a walk through of a systemic perspective of a family.

A Lens for Viewing the World out There

A family, any family, operates in three worlds. Roger Kaufman has described the three worlds: Mega, Macro, and Micro. The Mega World is the whole enchilada—the world at large. It is the global community and the ecosystems and the economic systems and the cultures. The influences of the Mega World on the family may seem as slight as the gentle waves of the ocean in front of a beach house. But the influences of the Mega World can be huge and inexorable, like the waves of the ocean pounding a beach house to smithereens during a Category 4 hurricane.

(The above passage is copied directly from Chapter 3, except that the word *family* replaces the word *organization* that appeared in Chapter 3. Organizations and families have much in common when viewed as systems.)

Families, businesses, and government agencies have in common that they all exist in the same global environment: They share the Mega World.[2] I grew up on a farm near a tiny community in western Kansas, right in the middle of the North American continent. It was easy to ignore the Mega World, most of the time. But the earliest memory of my life is of a Mega World event.

The Mega World event occurred on December 7, 1941, when I was four years old. The bombing of Pearl Harbor happened thousands and thousands of miles away, but it changed my life. A neighbor of mine was killed at Pearl Harbor, and several neighbors and members of my extended family died before World War II ended in 1946. The rationing of gasoline and sugar and tires and many other things had an impact. We even raised a few beans on our farm to support the war effort. (Armies travel on their stomachs; beans are cheap, filling, and easy to transport.) Even before

September 11, 2001, I knew that Mega World events were important to me and to my family.

We, all the persons and families in the world, share the Mega World. That is important and has consequences. For example, I had a housemate in graduate school many years after World War II. He was a Japanese man whose brother had been at Pearl Harbor— perhaps in the plane that dropped the bomb that killed my neighbor. The Mega World is not far away; it is next door or in your house. Switch on the television and you will see proof—perhaps more proof than you want.

On the other hand, the Macro World my family lives in is a much different Macro World than the Macro World for a family in Tokyo or Boston or Buenos Aires or Paris or Chengmai. Then, too, the Macro World for a business in Bird City, Kansas, is very different than the Macro World for a business in Naples or St. Petersburg or Cairo or New York City. The different Macro Worlds have their impact on families. My family speaks American English, not Cantonese. That is a fact, a consequence, a result, not a conscious choice. Yes, we could learn Cantonese, but it would not be easy because that language does not surround us. My family absorbs the culture around us; other families in other Macro Worlds absorb other cultures. We don't think about it, it just happens.

The Macro World of my family that I grew up in has strong influences on what I do over the course of weeks and months and years. But the Micro World had stronger influences on what I do every day. For example, interactions with my parents were much more influential than interactions with my teachers—especially the teachers I had as little to do with as possible!

The Micro World of your family is quite different than the Micro World of my family—I suppose. I haven't experienced your Micro World, so I could be wrong. The Micro World of some of the families I've worked with was very different than the Micro World of my family. The work I am thinking of was part of the Family and School Consultation Project sponsored by a mental health agency in Michigan. Some people said the families we worked with were dysfunctional, but that was silly. They were very functional! The problem was that the function was to produce behaviors that were considered dysfunctional outside that family. My point here is a simple one: the Micro World of families differs greatly between families *and* has very strong influences.

Here is another thought: I have often wished that Micro World influences were stronger to help me resist Macro World temptations and to help my children (and grandchildren) resist Macro World temptations. But the Macro World is bigger than the Micro World I can create and, in the long run, more powerful. The Mega and Macro and Micro Worlds are conflicted and confusing. As a family member, I would like to understand them better. If I were a family therapist, understanding all three of those worlds would be a key aspect of my job, if I aspired to competence in serving my clients well.

A Systemic Perspective: The Anatomy of Performance[3]

Please examine the Anatomy of Performance view of the Wilma-Wilber-Tammy-Tommy family in Figure 4.1. Just notice that the perspective for a family has the same "look" as the perspective for Acme Landscaping. The systemic look is similar; the *details* are vastly different.

The view shows that the family is surrounded by influences, some probably good, some probably bad. This worries Wilma and Wilber. On the other hand, Tommy is fascinated by the mysteries of the bad influences; Tammy is frightened by them, at least for now. Just as it does for Acme, the Anatomy of Performance view shows many of the out-of-our-control variables that define the potential strategic challenges and opportunities for the family. Wilber thinks of them as "threats," not "challenges," and worries about Tommy's tendency to think of them all as "opportunities."

Most of us have had more practice at defining desirable results for businesses than for families. Not so for Wilma. She is like an irrepressible Human Resource director talking about developing everybody in sight! She can articulate developmental goals for everyone, especially Tammy. "Tommy will be Tommy," she complains. "Wilber is a difficult case, but Tammy is developing quite nicely." (Besides, Wilma really feels, deep down, that Tommy can do no wrong—well, maybe a little wrong, but only in the boys-will-be-boys sense.)

Figure 4.1: A Family: Wilma, Wilber, Tammy, and Tommy

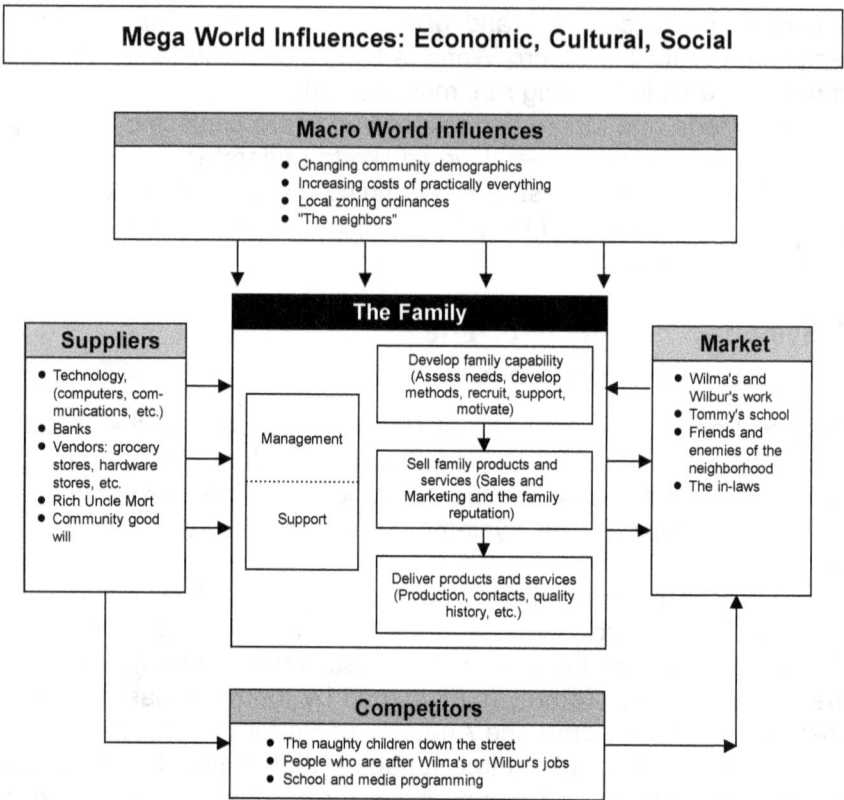

| Mega World Influences: Economic, Cultural, Social |

Macro World Influences
- Changing community demographics
- Increasing costs of practically everything
- Local zoning ordinances
- "The neighbors"

The Family

Suppliers
- Technology, (computers, communications, etc.)
- Banks
- Vendors: grocery stores, hardware stores, etc.
- Rich Uncle Mort
- Community good will

Management

Support

Develop family capability (Assess needs, develop methods, recruit, support, motivate)

Sell family products and services (Sales and Marketing and the family reputation)

Deliver products and services (Production, contacts, quality history, etc.)

Market
- Wilma's and Wilbur's work
- Tommy's school
- Friends and enemies of the neighborhood
- The in-laws

Competitors
- The naughty children down the street
- People who are after Wilma's or Wilbur's jobs
- School and media programming

Wilber thinks Tommy should start a lawn-mowing business. Wilma thinks Tommy is too young. The products and services of the family, right now, are provided by Wilma and Wilber when they go to work. They agree that the work of Tommy is really his school work, including the marks he earns (for better or worse) in citizenship. Wilma tells Wilber it isn't called "citizenship" anymore; Wilber tells Wilma that is one reason so many of Tommy's school friends will be juvenile delinquents. Wilma agrees, but will not admit it.

TIPS FOR ANALYSIS

The Macro World interactions for the family are the boundary-spanning interactions of the individual family members. They include making family purchases, earning paychecks, making donations to charities, participating in school-related activities, and the like. Macro World interactions are important for Wilma and Wilber.

How are you getting along with your suppliers, Wilma-Wilber?

"Decently. Some of them are raising prices, others are not; some are late with deliveries; others are not. My banker is happy at the moment, but my accountant is worrying and I do not know what will happen to us if the zoning boards and homeowners' associations keep changing their rules all the time."

How are you getting along at work, Wilma-Wilber?

"Really well. Wilma is doing a fabulous job! Oh, Wilber's boss complains vociferously all the time about everything, but he's been doing that for years and no one else wants to work for him, so he just has to keep Wilber. We are worried, though, that we aren't getting as many developmental opportunities as we want. And some of the people at work are just coasting. We wish they'd lead, follow, or get out of the way. Maybe some of them will get with the program soon. But maybe not."

What are the most serious challenges you face, Wilma-Wilber?

"Prices of everything we buy are going up, just as the children are getting into more expensive toys and school supplies and clothes and everything! The budget is getting squeezed. That's why I keep telling Wilma to watch the household expenses. And, yes, I know, Wilma keeps telling me to cut down on some of my toys. But that new lawn tractor isn't a toy! We worry about our jobs, especially the way the economy is and the way we don't really have much chance to develop at work. We are both thinking about going back to school. Yes. There are plenty of challenges to keep us awake at night right now, let alone when Tammy and Tommy hit those teen-age years."

Even if Wilma and Wilber could not articulate the strategic challenges readily, the Anatomy of Performance diagram would guide the analyst toward a comprehensive set of questions that would uncover the critical family issues they face. What is more, Wilma and Wilber would recognize the questions as important to the family. The Anatomy of Performance can uncover too many issues for Wilma or Wilber or any mere mortal to grasp clearly. The analyst can help sort and prioritize the issues by using the performance system perspective.

Another Systemic Perspective: The Total Performance System[4]

The mission statement in the TPS diagram in Figure 4.2 emphasizes mutual support. The support is for the growth and development of each family member. The support relates to multiple roles of each family member who has a role as person and a member of the larger community. The words of the mission statement connect not only to the marketplace (Macro World), but also into the Mega World. The words "contributing members of" connect to the value added to others in the extended neighborhood. As with a business, the words in a mission statement are meaningless unless family members make them meaningful. How? By helping one another do the work of the family, grow, and develop.

Figure 4.2: TPS Diagram

The Family

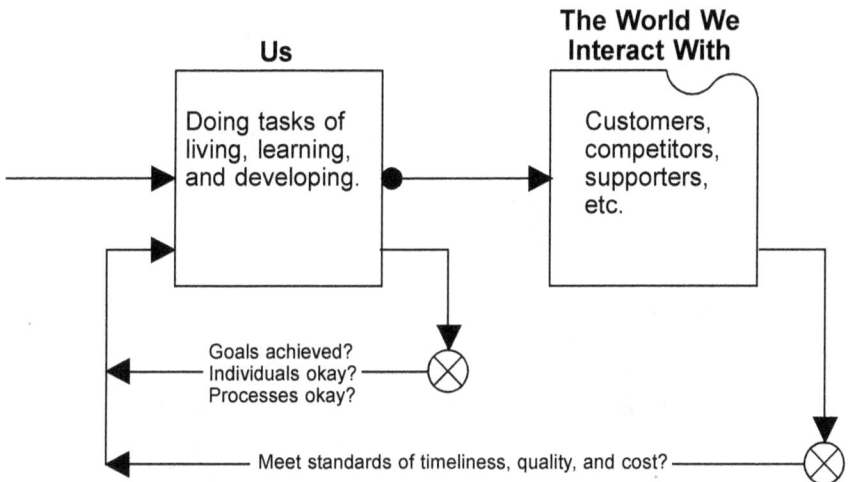

Goal Statement: Our family supports one another as we grow and develop as family members, persons, and contributing members of our neighborhood, workplaces, schools, and community.

Another Systemic Perspective: The Value-Adding Processes

One function of families in the Mega and Macro Worlds is to supply organizations with workers and governments with citizens. The work of the family in doing the tasks of daily living is not all that important from a societal perspective. On the other hand, the work of the family provides a huge number of opportunities for learning. Learning to do the tasks, learning to work together, learning to help one another, learning from one another. These learning experiences can be extraordinarily valuable to both children and parents. As Wilma puts it, "If I can teach Tommy something, and learn enough patience to do it, I can surely teach my assistant at work to do a few simple tasks!"

Wilber agrees, and asserts that both Tommy and her assistant should learn some self-management skills into the bargain. Wilma likes that notion. She hates supervising Tommy; she would rather hug him. And she hates supervising her assistant; she would rather scream at him.

Neither Wilma nor Wilber has drawn a picture that shows the work flow for the family. Perhaps that is because the work flow is not the main thing for the family, as it must be for a business. "Up in the morning, out on the job" about describes it for Wilber; Wilma uses a more complex procedure for getting ready to go to work.

Wilber sometimes says Wilma should be looking for a better paying job. He is right. (Just ask him!) Wilma says the job security she has now is worth a lot. She is right. (Just ask her!) Some families formalize the value-adding processes to some extent by acknowledging that "going to school" is a value-adding process for children and adults; as the world changes, people learn how to cope or excel, and a family is a support system for doing that.

Wilma and Wilber sometimes make lists of jobs to be done and explicitly demonstrate to Tommy and Tammy how to do them. Tommy teaches Tammy many useful things and not as many bad things as he could. He has even been known to cook a meal, following a plan that Wilma wrote down for him. And Wilber shows Tommy and Tammy how to do things like mow the lawn, take out the garbage, and (if Wilma is not looking) sweep trash off the sidewalk and under the hedge out of sight.

Wilma and Wilber know, sort of, how Tammy and Tommy are doing. They paid close attention when the children were infants, but sometimes they do not pay quite enough attention, now.

TIPS FOR ANALYSIS

In working with families having difficulties, I always encouraged them to be sure they knew how well each family member is progressing. We often developed specific "progress plotters" that were simple charts for tracking progress toward explicit little goals for the parents and for each child. As soon as noticing progress "came naturally" to people in the family, we stopped doing it explicitly—except when problems occurred, as they always did. Some of the healthiest families I know do the same.

A—probably *the*—major value-adding process in a family is modeling. Children imitate role models, for good or ill. Wilma frowns whenever Wilber says, "Do as I say, not as I do!" and encourages him to learn to live up to his good intentions. "You aren't perfect," she says, "and should not pretend to be. But you can be a good role model for the children by modeling continuous improvement!" (Wilber says she could do that too.)

Wilma and Wilber are the mentors and, just like it would help Wilber to have an effective mentor at work, it helps Tammy and Tommy if Wilma and Wilber are good mentors. John and Cindy, at Acme Landscaping, add enormous value by mentoring and teaching and nagging and otherwise supporting the development and performance of workers. Wilber and Wilma do the same in the family. Tommy models for Tammy, for good or ill. And, though he might not admit it, Tommy learns from Tammy.

Another Systemic Perspective: The Support Processes

Neither Wilber nor Wilma is an expert in family support processes. They absorbed a lot growing up, but do not "know what they know." They do know that Wilma's "intuitive reactions" are often different than Wilber's "gut reactions." That's a problem. Sometimes they can work out the differences easily, and sometimes Wilber says, "There are just some things Wilma isn't rational about." Wilma believes the same thing about Wilber. Both are right.

The support processes in the family are, in a sense, more important than support processes in a business. Supporting each family member in helping that person add value—or develop in order to do so—is the major societal function of families. Developing employees is not, currently, the major social function of businesses.

Support processes are essential in either a family or a business. Support processes in a business derive their value from making the value-adding processes less costly or better in some other way. The same might be true in a family, but it is not true in any obvious sense. But maybe Wilma fixes Wilber's meals to help him work long hours and not from force of habit, because she loves him, or because she likes to get him out of the house so that she can have an affair with the plumber. Family members claim to support others, regardless, and it seems that they might when we observe

family members seeking to support pedophiles and mass murderers. Businesses are more inclined, we might imagine, to dismiss
pedophiles and mass murderers. We do not know for sure; I have
yet to learn about a "work from you cell" program sponsored by any
business.

Another Systemic Perspective: The Performers

The performers? That's Wilma and Wilber and Tammy and Tommy.
If they were a big corporation, Wilma would probably be the chief
operating officer (the COO), and Wilber would probably be the chief
executive officer (the CEO), but that is not certain. If I were doing a
performance improvement analysis for the family, I might ask which
role each would take, not because it matters, but because role clarity is often important. Tammy and Tommy are "our little angels," the
tangible results that prove to Wilma that marrying Wilber was a
good thing to do. There are issues in the family:

"Clean the bathroom, Tammy." "Tommy is the one that made
the mess."

"Clear the table, Tommy." "Why do I have to do
everything? Why can't Tammy do something?"

Filling out a Human Performance System specification for
family members might not be necessary, but if there are many role
issues, a performance improvement analyst might use the HPS
diagram to analyze why they occur and help devise procedures to
improve matters.

Another Systemic Perspective: The Management Processes

Wilma sometimes complains:

"I have to do everything in this family! Pick up after Wilber
and Tommy. Tammy doesn't make near the messes Wilber
and Tommy do, and she is already learning how to pick up
after herself. Men are such slobs! Why can't you just see
what should be done and do it? It doesn't take a genius to
see when the beds should be made and the bathrooms
cleaned!"

Wilber sometimes complains:

> "My mother didn't teach me to do housework! I'm willing, but whenever I do something, you complain that I do not do it right! Besides that, who takes care of the yard? Who started your car for you when you couldn't? Get this through your head: It takes two of us to do the parenting! My brother is a single parent and…"

Wilma counters:

> "Yes, yes, I know! But we should be able to work together better to get everything done! Arguing about it does no good. Let's sit down this evening and make a plan!"

That evening:

> Just as they start to plan, Tammy runs in screaming, "Tommy just fell out of the tree! I think he broke something!" So off they go to the Emergency Room where Tammy's diagnosis is confirmed by X-rays: Tommy's arm is broken. Again.

The scenario illustrates two types of management failures, which I mentioned earlier:

1. One type is the type that is "out there" and due to interactions among weather and economics and state-of-the-art and so on—the type that management must know about and adjust to—the Macro and Mega World influences.

2. The other is the type that is "in here" (almost) under our control—the things that good managers and good performers can make happen in their Micro World.

Tommy's broken arm represents the "out there" category. If Tammy's teeth grow in crooked the way Wilma's did, it will be another "out there" event. If Wilber or Wilma loses a job or contracts a serious disease and can't work, it will be an "out there" issue. If prices outpace their income growth, it will be an "out there" issue—an issue that can occur. Count on it.

Having a planned procedure for getting Tommy to the Emergency Room (you never know with Tommy) is an "in here" management/parenting response. When I was growing up, my parents had such procedures, I suppose, or else invented them as required.

The first time I hired a baby sitter for my children, the sitter taught me that we should document the procedures.

TIPS FOR ANALYSIS

Look carefully at management procedures, especially if you want to consider "cultural" issues. Families have management procedures: some effective, some ineffective, some documented, some not. So, too, do businesses and government agencies. I think every government agency probably has 17 elves in the basement, writing procedures for the agency. Maybe I'm wrong about that. They might get the same result by writing tons of memos.

One thing that family therapists and counselors do is help families figure out how to share the work of running the family. Good family therapists are often "management consultants." Similarly, a management consultant I know named Jan was asked how she had learned so much about helping management teams work effectively. Jan replied: "Teaching fifth grade in Kalamazoo!" What's more, people believed her immediately!

It is the task of leadership in a family, business, or agency to know about the "out there" variables and devise goals and strategies for dealing with them. It is the task of parents and management to make the adjustments possible and then to ensure that the things "in here" that are (almost) controllable actually happen. To make them happen, parents and managers must ensure that everyone has the tools and feedback and incentives and goals and such that the Human Performance System for each person says the person should have.

One other thing: The "in here" variables should be aligned with the "out there" variables—aligned intelligently and aligned for survival and prosperity, both now and later.

A major task of leadership and management is to align Micro World variables with Macro World variables and with Mega World variables. Otherwise, the leading and managing could be working energetically, diligently, and unwisely to get people to go in the wrong direction.

Summary

A person or a family does things or performs. To make performance better, we must look beyond the person or the family. We must look at "the world out there." Why? Because, like it or not, the world out there provides the context for evaluating family performance. If we seek to improve—to add net value—we must look beyond the performance per se.

The tools described in Chapter 3 for businesses can also be applied to families. Taking a system view of families is a well-established and honored practice among those who study families. We can use specific tools such as the Anatomy of Performance diagram and the Total Performance System diagram to help improve performance of families and individuals within them.

The question "How do I add value?" is an important one for each member of the family. Adding value, especially for Wilber and Wilma, includes the work they do outside the family to earn the money to support the family. But the value Wilma and Wilber add also comes from interactions with one another and with Tommy and Tammy. If these Micro World interactions are healthy, they support the development of the skills and goals and aspirations and knowledge that Tommy and Tammy can use in the Macro World of the neighborhood and school. And these interactions model the sorts of interactions that are healthy and helpful in the Macro World.

The Macro World is now the source of opportunities and threats. So, too, is the Mega World. It is the source of opportunities and threats for Wilber and Wilma and, perhaps even more importantly, Tammy and Tommy. Ideally, the Micro World interactions in the family help all family members learn and practice the interactions necessary to survive and prosper in the sometimes frightening and sometimes beckoning Macro World, and the frightening and beckoning and mysterious and often remote Mega World.

The tasks involved in performance improvement for families and for family members are, necessarily, interconnected and can become quite complex. Witness the complexities of family courts and family counseling and political and religious and humanitarian concerns for the well-being of families in the United States, Latin America, Europe, the Middle East, and the Far East.

Endnotes

1. Many members of the International Association for Behavioral Analysis (http://www.abainternational.org) and the Organizational Behavior Management Network (http://www.obmnetwork.com/index_hi.html) understand and use functional analysis. To them, "functional analysis" means a careful and data-based set of methods for determining what function a specific behavior has. For example, the unusually obstreperous behavior of a worker might, upon examination, prove to be "political" in that she is running for an office in her union; another worker's excessive absences might not be about disliking the workplace, but about caring for his ailing children.

2. Kaufman, R. (2000). *Mega planning: Practical tools for organizational success.* Thousand Oaks, CA: Sage Publishing. See also the first book in this series, *Change, Choices, and Consequences: A Guide to Mega Thinking and Planning* (Amherst, MA: HRD Press, 2006).

3. A blank copy of Rummler's Anatomy of Performance diagram is included in Appendix A: Analysis Tools.

4. A blank copy of the Total Performance System diagram is included in Appendix A: Analysis Tools.

Section II
Specifying What Improvement Means

Wanting to make things better is a key ingredient in many, even most, theories of motivation. Why do you turn up the volume on your radio? To hear it better. Why do you tie your shoes? To keep them on your feet better. Why do you listen to and read the news? To be better informed. Good is good, and better is better, and better is what I want!

"Who wants to make things better?"

If you ask this question often and of a variety of individuals and a variety of audiences, what answer will you get most often? The most frequent answer will probably be some form of "I do! I want to make things better!" Most people want to make things better.

Here is why it is important for a performance improvement analyst to know: It tells us something very important about the motivation for change. The motivation for change is already there! We do not have to add it; we can guide it.

But there is a difficulty, an important difficulty, that masquerades as a motivational difficulty.

"Better" can mean many things to many people. "Better" can mean:

- The way we used to do it
- The way I say to do it
- Pie in the sky talk by managers who do not know what the heck they are talking about
- Better for you and worse for me
- Dead enemies
- A feather in your cap and a thorn in my foot
- Smarter customers
- Smarter managers
- Smarter employees
- Whatever is someone's hot button of the moment

If we are to make performance "better," it just makes sense to define improvement in terms of:

- Better for me
- Better for the business/family/agency
- Better for the customers/clients/investors
- Better for the employees/managers/executives

- Better for the community
- Better for the economy
- Better for the culture
- Better for society
- Better for the world

Or, as we say, "better for all the stakeholders." The grammatical connector is *and*, not *or*. Look for win-win, what's-in-it-for-me improvements. Add net value. To improve is:

- Not to take from Tommy to benefit Tammy
- Not to steal from one division to benefit another
- Not to rob Peter to pay Paul
- Not to play a zero sum game

"Better" is the motivator. Most stakeholders want to make it better. Finding "better" for as many different stakeholders as possible is the challenge to the analyst.

Did I tell you that *changing* performance is much easier than *improving* performance? Do you understand why? It is because many changes are not improvements! If they were, the prescription for improvement would always and everywhere be simple: Just change something! But it does not work that way:

- "I win, you lose!" is child's play.
- "I win, you lose" is for Arnold Schwartzenager action movies.
- "Everyone wins" is for Governor Schwartzenager.
- "Everyone wins" is worthy of very wise adults.

"Everyone wins" requires taking the ISPI systemic issues standard very seriously. We must not only "consider systemic issues," we must confront them and deal with them constructively. We must align the Micro, Macro, and Mega Worlds. We must align critical business/organization/family results with the world outside and with the world inside, that is, with Critical Work Process results and with Critical Job results. If we do not do all that, the parts of the organization will be unable to cooperate intelligently; hence, they are almost forced to work at cross-purposes.

Doing so takes work and enthusiasm and competence and cooperation and intelligence and good tools. This section focuses on using the tools to find "better," to find direction, to find improvements that add (net) value and to find improvements for the whole *and* the parts.

Want to know how to do it?

TIPS FOR ANALYSIS

The key to improvements that benefit multiple stakeholders: Build relationships and make the numbers!

Ensuring that changes improve results and ensuring that everyone wins require building good relationships. Ensuring that everyone wins and is, thereby, motivated is supported by making the right numbers!

Tracking the right numbers helps all stakeholders know that progress toward "better" is occuring. Tracking the right numbers helps all stakeholders stay intelligently motivated.

Chapters 5 and 6 will help you get even better at doing that than you already are.

Chapter 5
Anatomy of a Business:
Improving Relationships and
Making the Numbers

Overview: All About Relationships

People afflicted with an absence of assertiveness or with the arrogance of ignorance will not be successful analysts. Analyzing a business, family, agency, or other system is an intellectual challenge that requires asking good questions and collaborating with the client to make the answers meaningful.

Asking good questions is necessary. Getting answers to them is necessary. But that is not enough. The answers have to be organized simply, clearly, and in ways that motivate and guide the client to act.

The fact that businesses, families, and agencies are systems is a huge advantage. Any analyst can know a lot going in if he or she knows a small number of fundamental properties of living systems.

TIPS FOR ANALYSIS

Knowing about and applying a few significant properties of systems is the responsibility of any analyst who seeks to *improve* performance and do so intelligently.

This chapter illustrates again why knowing about the Mega and Macro Worlds[1, 2] is important in analyzing a request for performance improvement services. There are techniques for getting information about the client's perceptions of the Mega and Macro Worlds and linking performance improvement efforts to those worlds. Many of the analysis skills are, at heart, the skills of intelligent conversation.

TIPS FOR ANALYSIS

Some of the specific techniques are included in this book. Stop and think about them or move right on and come back to the tips later, as you see fit.

All the persons and organizations that do business with a business have an explicit stake in the performance of the business. Owners and employees have a very large stake. Customers and suppliers have a smaller stake. Customers often think (sometimes correctly) that they could buy elsewhere and do as well. Suppliers can sell their goods and services to other organizations. Lenders and investors have stakes of all different sizes as do competitors and allies. All are engaged in commerce, participating in value exchanges that affect the business itself.

TIPS FOR ANALYSIS

The Anatomy of Performance shows that a business (or agency or family) is surrounded by a larger world. It is surrounded by the system's suppliers and competitors and customers and owner/investors and the (largely) unpredictable influences of the Mega World beyond. Use the Anatomy of Performance diagram to help you capture and clarify some of the external influences.

A business survives longer if the value exchanges with stakeholders are mutually beneficial. The principle of mutual benefit is not difficult to understand and is very important. Please make note about the importance of mutually beneficial value exchanges; it is always an important issue for the long-term performance of any business we seek to help.

Value exchanges forge relationships. For some stakeholders, the monetary value exchanges are at the heart of the relationships; for others, sentiments and hopes, and common goals and common values are involved. The John and Cindy relationship was almost entirely about monetary value exchanges at first, but now there is an element of friendship. Some of Acme Landscaping's relationships developed from John's friendships. A few business relationships have developed into friendships. John believes that is as it should be. Commercial transactions are necessary and social interactions are important in any business.

Improving Relationships with the World Outside: Understanding and Analyzing Macro and Mega World Influences

The Macro World

John and Cindy, like other managers in other enterprises, use numbers to track value exchanges relevant to the commercial aspects of the business. Please think about each of these items until you understand the importance of each relationship John and Cindy track.

1. How many customers do we have? (What is the trend? Up, down, or steady?)

2. How many dollars do customers spend with us? (What is the trend?)

3. How many suppliers do we have? How many dollars do we spend with each? How well do they deliver on time and at quality? What are the price trends? (The answers provide important data for monitoring value exchanges.)

4. How many employees does it take to screw in a lightbulb or make a widget? What are our materials, labor, and overhead costs per unit sold?

5. What are the trends in employment costs and in labor productivity?

6. How is our cash flow, in and out? Should we borrow money? From which lenders?

TIPS FOR ANALYSIS

Ask yourself "What would happen if this number were to change?" **Ask clients these questions as part of every analysis you do.** If asking such questions is not part of your established role, ask them anyway, perhaps in casual conversations while waiting for elevators or waiting for meetings to begin. If you are talking to senior executives, they will almost certainly engage in the conversation; some lower-level managers or managers of support functions will not know the answers and will not engage.

John faces a perennial strategic issue:

> How can we be sure of supplies, yet minimize our inventory costs and maintain good relationships with our suppliers?

Cindy faces a perennial operations issue:

> Are we on track toward our goals/objectives/whatever we call them? Are we tracking the right numbers? Not too many, not too few, and at just the right time?

The fundamental business questions are all about relationships. That will come as a surprise to some hard-headed business people, especially in large organizations. But even the financial numbers are about relationships when we think about what the numbers really mean—and to whom. So too are the production numbers. Are we producing just enough to meet our customer requirements and fulfill our own financial requirements? We require the precision of numbers because the relationships are so important. But as an often-quoted (and misquoted) philosopher, Thomas Hobbes,[3] said: "Numbers are the counters of wise men and the money of fools." Numbers are the indicators of value, not the value itself. Mythical King Midas made that discovery on the way to self-destruction. Businesses who confuse a business necessity (profits) with business goals (maintaining good relationships with customers and other stakeholders) are on their way to self-destruction.

On the other hand, businesses and would-be performance improvers that forget about profits are actively courting destruction. Is that a surprise to you? It was to me. The part about businesses was not a surprise, but the part about performance improvers having to be concerned about profits was an unwelcome surprise. I was educated and trained in psychology, not in business. I just wanted to be the performance expert and remain blissfully ignorant of critical business issues like profitability. Not very smart. Had friends such as Geary Rummler not rescued me from such ignorance, I would have, deservedly, failed to be helpful many times.

Customer and supplier relationships are closely linked to the business. Many accounting numbers track closely linked relationships. And relationships are tracked by intuition when numbers are inadequate to inform business decisions.

TIPS FOR ANALYSIS

Use common sense, the Anatomy of Performance diagram, your experience, client body language, hesitations, and voiced concerns as your guide. Find out about key suppliers of money or referrals or key customers or employees or materials or services. Consider accounting and legal services and whatever else seems pertinent to the situation.

The Mega World

Mega World relationships are sometimes important, but some are *usually* not closely linked to a business. Changes in

- Climate or weather
- Social values and climate
- Political events
- Tactics or weaponry or desperation or enthusiasm of enemies

are always occurring, sometimes influential, and usually less predictable than how suppliers and customers will react.

Mega World relationships regularly, but unpredictably, become closely linked. A fire on the premises of a key customer or one of John's key customers declaring bankruptcy can have a major impact. That is why far-seeing executives keep a close eye on Mega World events and look for numbers and trends that might make the Mega World influences more predictable or at least less dramatic and disastrous. Getting the building blown up by terrorists will certainly be dramatic if it happens, but if all the business or agency records are backed up and stored elsewhere, the consequences will be less disastrous—to the people who survive. Mega World induced disasters tend to clarify boundaries between friends and enemies.

TIPS FOR ANALYSIS

An analyst should get the client's views about the Mega World. What important events are occurring there that might have strategic implications. Seek clues as to what the client values, the client's hopes and dreams and fears. Direct or clumsy questioning might make the client uncomfortable and wonder what that has to do with anything, but at the right moment and in the right place, clients will talk readily about Mega World issues. Timing is important.

Critical Business Issues: Relationships between Acme Landscaping and the World Outside

The attention of managers and executives, in general, tends to move as the business grows:

- From satisfying one key customer (the one in front of them),
- To satisfying many customers,
- To satisfying customers-yet-unknown.

The pattern is to move from close in to farther out, from the central parts of the Anatomy of Performance diagram to the surrounding world. Consider the situation with Acme Landscaping. John spends more and more of his time focused on the world outside, now that Cindy is onboard to manage much of the work. Cindy was not interested in that world and is happier now that she knows John is tracking it. She focuses on delivery of landscaping services and leaves the entire rest of the world up to John.

Remember the Acme mission statement?

Acme Home Landscaping provides landscaping services to builders and buyers that add attractiveness to fine homes, thereby enhancing the beauty and the economy of the neighborhood.

John is getting increasingly serious about measuring some of the Mega World influences (enhancing the beauty and the economy of the neighborhood) that he barely had time to think about before. He is slowly learning that the neighborhood is bigger than he thought it was. He is forming new relationships. He gets a referral now and then from people he met at a national landscaping conference.

John likes to say, "I don't lose customers when someone moves out of state, I just refer them to a friend." Cindy wishes John's out-of-state friends would refer more customers to Acme. John says they will as he and Cindy learn how to appeal to the out-of-state customers' tastes with landscaping that works locally. Cindy thinks John spends too much time going to conferences and such; John worries about that and fears he does not go enough. That is why he tracks referrals and potential referral sources carefully.

TIPS FOR ANALYSIS

Mission statements are good sources of information and good conversation starters. Quote a word or phrase and ask, "What does that mean to people around here?" and, later on, "What does it mean to you?" Or ask, "How would you know if that is happening?" and, later on, "Should we be tracking that?"

Another tactic is to lead an exercise that helps people generate mission statements. One such exercise and a tool for doing it is included in Appendix A. An analyst can learn a lot about business issues, cultures, and sacred cows that way. Just do the exercise, watch, listen, and learn. Take notes, too, maybe on a blank Total Performance System diagram, as I do, or on a blank Anatomy of Performance diagram, as Geary Rummler does.

Improving Relationships within the Organization

John is concerned with the Macro World and, increasingly, the Mega World. The Micro World of Acme is now primarily Cindy's domain. Cindy is learning how to take the initiative and keep John informed. John is learning how to listen and respond and share ideas without meddling. Slowly but surely, they are learning to differentiate between executive functions and management functions. Not in theory—they do not think about theory. They just think about making Acme Landscaping successful.

Each is responsible for making specific numbers. Both know they have to work together as a team, but each takes on responsibility for tracking specific numbers and acting on the data. Taking on responsibility for specific numbers is one way they separate and differentiate roles, make sure nothing falls through the cracks, and integrate everything about Acme. Cindy watches cash flow and tracks profit margin per job, customer satisfaction, on-time delivery, and labor costs. John also tracks cash flow and how the work flows in, especially from new referral sources or from members of community groups that he belongs to. He watches everything Cindy tracks and is getting better at coaching rather than meddling the way he did at first.

TIPS FOR ANALYSIS

Good questions to ask, often and repeatedly, of executives and managers and supervisors include: "How do you know how well things are going?" and "What numbers do you look at to tell you how things are going?"

Critical Process Issues: Measurable Objectives and Performance Criteria

John and Cindy make up both the leadership/executive team and the management team. In much larger organizations, those functions are more separated, leaving even more opportunities for miscommunication, misunderstanding, conflict, and infighting.

There is much to do to set realistic objectives and to meet them "the Acme way." Before telling you a bit about how that works, let me just mention an oddity of the English vocabulary here. Skip the next two paragraphs if you are not interested in such matters.

Executives do not *execute* very much. Executives lead. Managers manage, they do not execute the value-adding work. The people who trim the shrubs and dig the dirt and plant the flowers and listen actively to customers are the ones who execute.

- Leadership defines what must be executed.

- Management organizes, supports, and guides so that the work can be accomplished and managed.

- Workers do the work; workers execute the leadership plans and management policies.

In Acme, both John and Cindy grab a shovel now and then, helping to execute their own executive and management decisions! John also executes loans and Cindy executes contracts with clients. They model good work performance. They are also intelligent enough to get input from the landscaper workers when they formulate plans and make decisions.

Not every executive or manager should model work performance, even if competent to do so. It is usually a better tactic (and sometimes a necessary tactic) to have others model the desired performance. John and Cindy do it in Acme Landscaping because there is not a professional support staff of trainers and such, and because sharp differentiation of roles is not necessary. A little differentiation is what makes coordination of the work possible.

Now, back to Acme Landscaping. Cindy might have confided to John when they first met that she wasn't comfortable setting business goals and writing down performance standards.

John commented, "Cindy, I do not set the business goals or the performance standards. My banker and my accountant do that." He went on to explain that he and the banker talked about how much he would have to grow the business to either sell it or feel secure about having enough customers to generate the cash to stay in business. Then he and the accountant talked about cash flow and profit margins and such. John discovered, through those conversations, what the economics of the business *must* look like if he is to stay in business. He often did not like what he learned, but he really likes the landscaping. He just had to work hard to get the numbers to line up.

Cindy said, "I think your standards had more to do with our success than those conversations with bankers and accountants. You have higher standards for our work than many landscapers do."

John said he could not take much credit for that. "The customers set the standards. If I had a reputation for sloppy work, they wouldn't buy."

Cindy did not entirely believe John about the standards. But what he said was true. He has a good eye for landscaping, but if he tries to do the work too well, it costs more than customers will buy. If he cuts corners to cut costs and lower prices, fewer customers will buy the lesser quality work. John strikes a balance. As he puts it: "I'd like to make every job into something to publish articles and pictures about in landscaping magazines. Once I had a client who wanted her home to be featured in a magazine. I loved doing that work! But usually that is not the client's goal and it cannot be Acme's goal. As I said, the customers set the standards."

Cindy argued, "You did too, John! You set the standards. You chose the market niche you work in, a niche where your standards match the standards of the buying public!"

John agreed that he had something to do with it, but he pointed out, "My banker and my accountant did that. They told me how much cash we had to earn from customers. All I did was find a market niche that might possibly generate that cash."

Cindy said, "That's all you did? That's more than I could do!"

The truth of the matter is that successful businesses strike a balance between what they would like to sell and what customers would like to buy. Staying in business requires that they continue to strike that dynamic balance. Such is the nature of business relationships (personal relationships, too). It sometimes feels to John and Cindy like walking a tight rope; it is a matter of striking the right balance most of the time, if not all the time.

Managing a successful business *is* a balancing act, striking balances among an array of systemic variables. A would-be performance improver whose only talent is improving one performance at a time is just competent enough to be dangerous. I know that from personal experience: Early in my career, my talent was improving one performance at a time; I was lucky enough to find a few clients who knew that they must focus on balancing *several variables at once and all the time*. One client told me I knew just enough to be dangerous! I was angry; he was right.

TIPS FOR ANALYSIS

Any time a client begins saying things that you can link to the balancing act or relate, in your own thinking, to the subsystem maximization principle,[4] turn on your active listening skills and follow up on it. The point often comes up in the context of talking about internal conflicts between people or departments. Ask questions about the business issues related to the conflicts. I sometimes signal a shift in topic: "That's fascinating! Could we talk about it a little bit?" The explicit shift provides a natural way to return to the main topic: "That was really informative! I'd like to know more about that, but I think we should get back to what we were talking about before, okay? Or do you have something else you want to say now?"

The Performance Analysis Lens: Aligning Critical Business Issues, Critical Process Issues, and Critical Job Issues[5]

Let us take a bit of time to look back at what we know about Acme Landscaping and Wilma and Willie's family and many other systems. Consider this question:

How might an analyst get the right information to improve important performances at Acme (or anywhere else)?

The analyst is *looking at* the surface structure of a business, seeing it through the client's eyes. The analyst is *looking for* the deep structure variables—the variables that generate what anyone can see. The analyst knows that each person sees a slightly different surface structure. That is as it should be; it is as it must be. The analyst is trying to put together a clear and simple picture or view or consensus perspective that can be used to guide action.

TIPS FOR ANALYSIS

Here is a secret—a secret only because most overlook it:

Analysis for performance improvement is much more about synthesis than analysis: It is putting together the bits and pieces so that all can see them clearly.

Tools such as flowcharts, the Total Performance System diagram, the Anatomy of Performance diagram, the Human Performance System diagram, and the Organizational Elements Model are useful for two reasons. They help the analyst:

- Sort through mounds of surface level data to find critical information

- Help the clients understand and use the findings

If you have a tool you like that does not do both things, get rid of it as soon as you can. It creates an extra step in the analysis process—an opportunity for confusion and error. Find another tool that will do whatever that tool now does for you and helps sort and organize.

John and Cindy are intelligent enough to appreciate a really fine analysis, but what they can actually use is a diagram or sketch or mental model that allows them to see, feel, and manage the business. Performance analysts would do well to heed the words of Nobel Laureate Georg von Bekesy[6] who said: "First you make the analysis. Then you make the synthesis. The synthesis tells you if the analysis was right."

Dr. von Bekesy earned the Nobel prize, in large measure, for his pioneering effort to construct a realistic model that replicated basic phenomena in the research on hearing. Von Bekesy's words, uttered in a colloquium at Harvard when I was a graduate student there, solved a huge problem for me—a problem I did not know even existed until I encountered it several times years later.

How do you know when an analysis is "good enough"?

How do you know the findings are accurate enough and complete enough to be worth something to the client?

That might be nice to know, would it not, when you begin an analysis? When you plan the analysis project? So you do not just collect tons of data and take tons of time and then give the client a big bill, a big report, and a headache? So you do not exemplify analysis paralysis in its most virulent form? So you do not collect more and more data because you haven't a clue what information is actually required in that organization by that set of clients at that particular time?

Here is the answer to "How do I know when it is good enough?"

TIPS FOR ANALYSIS

An analysis is good enough when it shows (the client) exactly what must be done to improve performance and exactly why that performance is worth improving.

How many times have you reported an analysis, observation, or opinion and been asked, "So what do you want me to do about it?" It takes both knowledge and skill to quickly reach the point at which the client knows what to do.

It pains me to say it, but there are people who have been in our field for many years who have yet to reach that point even once, let alone routinely! They do not lack intelligence or motivation or good intentions. They lack just a few methods and tools that they could readily learn to use.

If you wanted to be in their ranks, you would not be reading this book.

So let us get on with it. What are the tools and methods?

You have already seen three of the main ones:

1. The Anatomy of Performance diagram[7]
2. The Total Performance System diagram[8, 9, 10]
3. The Human Performance System diagram[11]

The Human Performance System diagram and the Total Performance System diagram always look about like the examples of diagrams you have seen. The Anatomy of Performance diagram comes in several variations, each tailored to a specific set of systemic issues. It always shows the basic parts of the anatomy that you have seen, but it is sometimes tailored to show additional details of specific sets of systemic issues.

Maybe I should not tell you this for fear that it might confuse you, but the three tools above are all the same tool! They are variants of the same thing; they are diagrams that show adaptive systems. They are all pictures of the elephant—the adaptive system. Each is just a slightly different view that clarifies specific issues.

If you have read other books in this series, you have also seen examples of a fourth really important tool, Kaufman's Organizational Elements Model, which features the Mega, Macro, and Micro worlds. The tools are dealt with more thoroughly in other books in the series and mentioned here for your convenience.

Another tool that is often useful is the flowchart, especially one drawn to show cross-functional relationships.[12] The cross-functional map reminds people of swim lanes in an Olympic pool. Each person/department that affects the process is shown as a row (swim lane). The flow of the work is shown by an ordinary flowchart, ordinary except the parts performed in each swim lane are shown in the appropriate swim lane.

TIPS FOR ANALYSIS

If you want to be competent, quick, and thorough as an analyst, please do yourself a favor and get good at using cross-functional maps. If you are moderately adept at flowcharting, you can learn to make cross-functional maps by redrawing a flowchart or two into swim-lane format. A side benefit of doing so is that it makes it easier to validate the flowchart. Owners of each swim lane can quickly find their parts of the chart and tell you whether or not it accurately describes what they do.

After you have validated the cross-functional map with each row owner, it is still wise to bring them all together to discuss the map. Why? Because they invariably find ways to simplify the work flow and thereby improve the reliability and reduce the cost of the work! You know you are doing it correctly if people's first reaction is "No, that can't be the way we do it!" and their second reaction is "We have to change that!"

This effect of using cross-functional maps yielded the jargon "is-map" and "should-map." Is-maps provide motivation for developing, agreeing upon, and implementing should-maps. I tried making should-maps myself, as an analyst, but I rarely could get clients enthusiastic about the maps I made, especially if I made should-maps that were clear, clean, and feasible. People would often look at the should-map and say, "That is how we do it now." Believing they were already doing it, they continued using the messy process that an is-map would have shown them! After thinking to myself about how stupid they were, I got over it and stopped being such a stupid analyst.

The flowchart, especially the cross-functional version, is a powerful tool, well described in many books and articles, and familiar to many people in our field, in the quality arena, and in several specialties in engineering.

TIPS FOR ANALYSIS

The cross-functional map is very useful for aligning the work and the workers with the organization. Imagine that you have a "should-map" for the major work processes ("This is the way we should do each landscaping project at Acme"). Imagine that each person, including John and Cindy, knows how his or her work contributes to that work flow. To make sure everyone knows and has the same mental image, draw a "swim lane" for John, a "swim lane" for Cindy, and "swim lanes" for each of the workers. If you do it correctly, each swim lane shows how each person contributes to the work flow. You can draw the swim lanes now just to practice, but please remember that if you were consulting with John and Cindy, you would do it *with* them. You might draw a rough draft yourself and then have them validate and improve it.

Experts make drafts and work with clients to clarify and confirm them. It is one way to apply ISPI's Collaboration Standard.

There are also several project management tools that can be helpful. I will not describe them here because you probably know them better than I do. If not, they are widely available. What they do is help you keep things from falling through the cracks. They do little to help figure out what should be done or why.

Summary

Two fundamental issues are about relationships and can be managed best if numbers are used:

1. A strategy implementation issue: How can we be sure of supplies, yet minimize our inventory costs and maintain good relationships with our suppliers?

2. An operations issue: Are we on track toward our goals/objectives/whatever we call them? Are we tracking the right numbers? Not too many, not too few, and at just the right time?

A wise analyst will probe to get information about these two perennial critical business issues during the analysis. Even if the matter under analysis seems to be far removed from these issues, it is not. On the other hand, if the matter under analysis is actually far removed from these issues, it is almost certain to be trivial and not worth pursuing.

Customer and supplier issues are always relevant and usually a matter of immediate concern for an analysis directed toward performance improvement. Mega World issues are always relevant and always important for strategic planning; however, Mega World issues are often not of immediate concern for current operations until after it is too late to deal with them well. (That's why we should plan ahead with a view toward social, economic, political, and cultural issues.)

Managers (like Cindy) are often concerned with cost-saving issues. Executives (like John) might worry about current costs, but their focus is and should be strategic. (That is why executives do not get as excited as managers about cost savings; then, too, most executives have encountered bogus cost-savings data and have learned to be skeptical about it.)

TIPS FOR ANALYSIS

If you want to capture an executive's attention, focus on critical business issues. I know I've uncovered a critical business issue during an analysis, because critical business issues tend to capture executive attention. They listen actively and discuss them energetically.

Many critical business goals or objectives or standards or whatever are set in accord with external realities and constraints. It is important to know about those external realities and constraints when setting performance improvement targets.

An analysis is "good" if and only if it helps executives and/or managers understand what should be done, why, and how it can be accomplished. Accuracy and completeness are nice.

Analysis tools such as the Total Performance System diagram, the Anatomy of Performance diagram, the Human Performance System diagram, the Organizational Elements Model, cross-functional maps, or the Mission Statement Job Aid are useful because they help the analyst quickly discover, understand, and communicate critical information to clients.[13] Organizational goals are set with a view toward external constraints, opportunities, and threats. Micro World goals are set in that context and with a view toward internal constraints, opportunities, and threats.

Endnotes

1. Kaufman, R. (1998). *Strategic thinking: A guide to identifying and solving problems.* Arlington, VA & Washington, D.C.: Jointly published by the American Society for Training & Development and the International Society for Performance Improvement.

2. Watkins, R. (2000). Is distance learning right for your organization? http://pignc-ispi.com/articles/distance/isdistance.htm

3. Hobbes, T. (1651). Leviathan. Available online at: http://www.infidels. org/library/historical/thomas_hobbes/leviathan.html

4. Subsystem maximization principle: It is impossible to maximize the functioning of a total system and a subsystem at the same time. Readers interested in more information are invited to do an Internet search on "subsystem maximization principle." It is an extremely important concept and principle.

5. Critical Business Issues (CBIs) are "keep executives awake at night" issues related to organizational performance, especially threats to survival or strategic opportunities. Critical Process Issues (CPIs) are about the means of providing products and services to achieve operational and strategic goals. Critical Job Issues (CJIs) are about the tasks managers and workers must perform to ensure that the critical processes meet the challenges of the critical business issues. Rummler discusses CBI, CPI, and CJI linkages in Rummler, G. A. (1998). The three levels of alignment, in *Moving from training to performance*, Robinson and Robinson (Eds.) San Francisco, CA: ASTD and Berrett-Koehler Publishers. And in Rummler, G. A. (2004). *Serious performance consulting: According to Rummler.* Silver Springs, MD: International Society for Performance Improvement.

6. von Bekesy, G. (circa 1960). Personal communication.

7. Rummler, G. A. (2004). *Serious performance consulting: According to Rummler.* Silver Springs, MD: International Society for Performance Improvement.

8. LaFleur, D., & Brethower, D. M. (1998). *The transformation: Business strategies for the 21st century.* Grand Rapids, MI: Impact Groupworks.

9. Malott, M. (2001). *Paradoja de Cambio Organizacional.* Editorial Tillas.

10. Malott, M. (2003). *Paradox of Organizational Change.* Reno, Nevada:Context Press.

11. Rummler, G. A., & Brache, A. P. (1995). *Improving performance: How to manage the white space on the organization chart* (2nd Ed.). San Francisco, CA: Jossey-Bass.

12. A template for drawing cross-functional maps is included in the newer versions of Microsoft Visio Professional.

13. Blank copies of some of these tools can be found in Appendix A.

Chapter 6
Anatomy of a Family:
Improving Relationships

Overview: All About Relationships

It is easy to believe that a family is all about relationships. Just listen to people talk at a family reunion: "Is Cousin Barbara still married to that dimwit?" "Do Uncle X and Aunt Y keep in touch with you now that they are living in Pennsylvania?" and so on. Using families as a model, we can generalize the concept of relationships to larger and even larger organizations. Much conversation will be about relationships. Consider the most animated conversations; some part of them will be about relationships.

The same is true for business conversations. Many will be about relationships with suppliers, customers, or competitors; about relationships between departments; and relationships between people.

"Why do you think Monica never comes to these family gatherings?" "Is Cousin Eloise still running with that wild crowd?" "When will Uncle George's cousin get out of jail?" "Is it true that Edgar lost his job?" "Is Wilber still going to college?" There are many conversations about how family members are relating to the Macro World of the family as a whole and to the Mega World outside the family.

TIPS FOR ANALYSIS

Get in the habit of listening for issues about relationships. If you are already good at that, get good at identifying the stated or implied value exchanges that are related to the relationships.

Listen to the talk:

- Who is officious Aunt Millicent complaining about now?
- What else are people in the family talking about?

(continued)

TIPS FOR ANALYSIS (concluded)

- Are they concerned that if Cousin Eloise keeps running with the wrong crowd there is little hope she'll deal with her addiction problem?

- Are they concerned that if Edgar keeps losing jobs he won't be able to pay his bills?

- Are they happy that Wilbur is gaining knowledge that will help him economically and socially?

- Are they concerned that Uncle George's cousin broke a law of society and must pay the price by serving jail time?

- Are they aware that when he gets out he might require emotional support from the family?

Improving Relationships with the World Outside: Understanding and Analyzing Macro and Mega World Influences

The Macro World

Wilma and Wilber, like other parents, use numbers to track value exchanges relevant to family financial matters—the commercial aspects of the family. Please think about each of the items until you understand the importance of each relationship they track and why they are wise to track it:

- How many sources of income do we have?

- How much money comes from each source?

- How many bills do we have to pay? How many dollars do we spend with each? How well does each deliver on time and at quality? What are the price trends? (The answers provide important data for monitoring value exchanges.)

- How much does it cost for the expenses of each family member? For each major budget category? What are the trends—increasing or decreasing or projected?

- How is our cash flow, in and out? Should we borrow money? From which lenders?

To be honest, Wilma and Wilber sometimes use guesses rather than actual numbers to track these relationships. They also tend to procrastinate about reviewing the status of the numbers. They feel a little guilty about that, but haven't done anything to improve their management of financial resources. Wilber says, "If I had more money, I'd manage it carefully!" (Wilma says, "Yeah, right.")

Wilma and Wilber face a perennial strategic issue:

How can we be sure of the necessities, yet minimize our costs, pay our bills, and save for the future?

Unlike governments, they cannot just raise taxes. They do the equivalent a bit too much, and borrow more money than they should, each time resolving to be more prudent next time. They also think about asking for raises and getting more knowledge and experience to justify the raises.

They also face an operations issue, made more severe by their tendency to use "guesstimates" rather than actual numbers in their financial planning:

Are we on track toward our goals/objectives/whatever we call them? Are we tracking the right numbers? Not too many, not too few, and at just the right time?

Wilma and Wilber know clearly that their family is not about money—they could both probably earn more money if that were their sole responsibility. They know they make financial sacrifices for the family and do so quite willingly, except in occasional weak moments. "If I hadn't married you and had these babies, I could afford a new dress. And I'd still be getting expensive presents from admirers," thinks Wilma. Wilber's moments of weakness are more focused on vehicles than clothes. The family is not about money, but as in many families, many of their arguments are about money. "If you hadn't bought that new washing machine, we could send Tommy to camp." It is a version of "If we can send a man to the moon, we can surely afford to spend more on bicycle paths."

The Mega World

Mega World relationships are sometimes important, but are no more closely linked in families than in businesses. Changes in climate or weather, social values and climate, political events, and tactics or weaponry or desperation or enthusiasm of enemies are always occurring, sometimes influential, and usually less predictable than Macro World happenings.

Mega World relationships regularly, but unpredictably, become closely linked. A cold winter or a hot summer influences utility bills and tempers. Wilma and Wilber think of themselves as liberals, but they do not have liberal attitudes toward some of the children in the neighborhood who are mean to Tammy and Tommy or who try to get them to do forbidden activities. If the man who regularly visits the registered sex offender a half mile away begins to show interest in Tammy or Tommy, Wilber and Wilma get uptight. Then there are all those television programs and the places Tommy keeps finding on the Internet! Like many other parents in many other times, Wilma and Wilber can recite chapter and verse about how the world is going downhill. The Mega World affects the family and is a bit frightening; Wilma and Wilber (and even Tommy and Tammy) know they cannot control important Mega World events and trends. (Tommy and Tammy sometimes think Wilma and Wilber **are** the Mega World; parents represent it, perhaps well, but never completely.)

Critical Family Issues: Relationships
with the World Outside

Wilma and Wilber are always concerned about worldly influences. Their concern grows as Tammy and Tommy grow. They move from loosely monitoring Tammy and Tommy as they play in the yard to closely monitoring (or just worrying) about them as they go farther out into the neighborhood and beyond. As Tammy and Tommy grow older, they will, increasingly, run errands, attend school-sponsored events, and even go on field trips with scout troops and church groups.

The pattern is to move from close in to farther out, from the central parts of the Anatomy of Performance diagram to the surrounding world. That pattern is clear, not only from what we know about families in general, but from the goal statement of their family:

> Our family supports one another as we grow and develop
> as family members, persons, and contributing members of
> our neighborhood, workplaces, schools, and community.

What Wilma and Wilber and Tammy and Tommy do to support one another changes markedly with changes in the world outside and changes in the age, knowledge, and aspirations of each member of the family of four.

Improving Relationships within the Family

The Micro World of the family might have been Wilma's domain in years gone by, but roles have changed. Both parents work outside the family, sharing responsibility, sharing decision making, and sharing anguish. Both grew up in a world in which the family roles were different. The roles modeled by their parents do not fit the family Wilma and Wilber experience. Wilma is learning a lot about how her father viewed the world and how Wilber views it now. Wilber understands his mother much better than he did and hopes not to make all the mistakes his father did.

Slowly but surely, Wilma and Wilber are learning to differentiate between issues related to the world outside and issues related to the world inside the family. They do not think about theory; they just think about making the family and all its members successful.

Both know they have to work together as a team, but each takes on responsibility for keeping track of specific issues and fulfilling specific responsibilities. Their roles are not defined by gender, but by the work each must accomplish to ensure a happy and healthy family. Their roles are differentiated, but no matter how they differentiate roles, they must work together to make sure nothing falls through the cracks. Blaming one another for failures is destructive. Working together to resolve or prevent problems is constructive. Just as a mature and productive business team establishes roles but ignores roles when necessary to get the work done, Wilma and Wilber have established roles but ignore the roles and help one another when necessary. Or at least, they always *say* they do that and usually try.

Critical Process Issues: Measurable Objectives and Performance Criteria

Wilma and Wilber make up both the leadership/executive team and the management team. They also do most of the work. They look forward to the day when Tammy and Tommy can do more. But they look on that day with mixed emotions. Unlike a business that tries to keep good workers working, the family mission is to enable family members to function well outside the family. In Tammy's and Tommy's case, that means leaving the family home! They might not leave at an emotional level, but certainly will not be there for mundane activities such as taking out the garbage and creating messes.

There is much to do to set realistic objectives and to meet them "our family's way." Both the objectives and the means of achieving them are expressions of and influenced by the family's values, whether or not the values, objectives, and means are written down anywhere or even talked about consistently

Values, in turn, are influenced by worldly matters. That is one reason Wilber and Wilma worry about the friendships Tommy and Tammy form, the television programs they watch, the Internet sites they visit, and the books or magazines or newspapers they will read. Wilma and Wilber seek to strike a realistic balance among competing values, including the values they absorbed from their parents and the values they seek to share with Tammy and Tommy.

Wilma resisted setting specific and measured objectives for the children's development. She thought that was cold. "Tammy does not develop on a schedule!" she asserted. "She develops at her own pace and in her own way." And, when Wilma complained about how much money they earned, Wilber did not counter by setting measured goals. As John said about the landscaping business, "Cindy, I do not set the business goals or the performance standards. My banker and my accountant do that." Wilber says, "Wilma, I do not set my salary, my boss and the business do that."

Wilber has gotten more comfortable about setting measured goals for their joint income even though much of that is beyond his and Wilma's control. But he is no more enthusiastic than Wilma about setting such goals within the family. He and Wilma regard their resistance as "protecting the children's childhoods" and assert that children should be allowed to be children.

Wilma shifted her views slightly when she attended a class about child development. She learned to think about helping the children develop the knowledge and skill sets Tommy and Tammy would benefit from as adults. Both Wilma and Wilber could get enthusiastic about helping the children develop self-management skills. They knew how hard it was to become self-reliant themselves when they started their first jobs and especially when they started the family. They believe it is important to help the children develop the skills necessary to be self-reliant. They like that a lot better than the prospect of perpetually nagging the children to "pick up your socks" or "eat your vegetables" or "be nice to your sister" and things like that.

They call their favorite development area the "Play Nicely with Others" series. It began as an effort to get Tammy and Tommy to fight less and "play nicely" together more. The short-term measures were the number of altercations per day, and the near-term measures were amount of time "playing nicely" per day and the number of activities they enjoyed doing together. Wilma and Wilber took turns tracking the data. Over time, they delegated the data tracking to Tommy and Tammy. And, over time, they neglected the data, unless something went wrong (it always did).

When the first "play nicely" project was initiated, it only took a week or so before Tommy heard Wilber and Wilma arguing and told them they should do a "play nicely" project. They did. (Wilber, without telling anyone, started a "play nicely" project himself at work. The goal was to get along better with another person there who Wilber considered a royal pain in the you-know-what.)

Why does an analyst have to know these things about personal development within the family? Because these are the issues facing family members.

Trying to "help" without knowing the issues is as foolish for a familial intervention as it is for a business intervention. It takes work to improve, whether you are part of a family or of a work team. The analyst must find out which issues are most salient and most urgent and most important. Which issues are those? For a family, it will be the issues that relate to the outside world, to the children's schoolwork to the parents' workplace, or to the extended family. For a business, it will also be the issues that relate to the outside world, such as customer service or sales and marketing or strategic relationships or relationships with suppliers.

TIPS FOR ANALYSIS

The point to notice is that the same systemic variables apply to both businesses and families. The specific content varies from business to business and family to family, but the content is important due to its relationship to the systemic variables.

The Performance Analysis Lens: Aligning Critical Business/Family Issues, Critical Process Issues, and Critical Job/Personal Development Issues

A quotation from Chapter 5 is repeated here with the word *business* changed to the word *family:* "The analyst is *looking at* the surface structure of a family, seeing it through the client's eyes. The analyst is *looking for* the deep structure variables, the variables that generate what anyone can see. The analyst knows that each person sees a slightly different surface structure. That is as it should be; it is as it must be. The analyst is trying to put together a clear and simple picture or view or consensus perspective that can be used to guide action."

Both businesses and families are systems. Knowing the key systemic properties enables the analyst to find the important issues quickly. More importantly, knowing the systemic properties enables the analyst to know in advance just how the issues must be dealt with.

You know, from your experience in a family, that everything is connected to everything else. If Wilma gets a raise, it influences the whole family. If Wilber loses his job or develops a gambling habit, it influences the whole family. If Tommy gets caught shoplifting or earns a scholarship to camp, it influences the whole family. If Tammy withdraws and stops talking to others, it influences the whole family. Surface structure events are visible. The deep structure causes are less visible and more important for purposes of analysis.

In what sense are deep structure causes more important? Deep structure variables influence not just one or two, but a whole array of surface events. And each surface structure event interacts with the relevant deep structure variables. Wilma did not fail to get the raise because of just one thing she did, nor did Tammy withdraw because of just one thing. Wilber would not start gambling because of just one thing, but because of a combination of many things. The same would be true for Tommy's shoplifting ineptitude or scouting prowess.

When Sigmund Freud developed the metaphor of the unconscious mind, he opened a way to think of deep structure variables as strange, mysterious, and almost unfathomable. He did not think of them that way, but too many others, following his lead, seemed to delight in the mysteriousness of the unconscious mind metaphor. Freud showed, time and time again, that the "mysterious" action of the unconscious mind was not at all mysterious once the analyst discovered the variables that lead up to the actions.[1] In other words, once we understand the variables, the behavior is no longer mysterious. So too it is with the variables that support development of persons in families and workers in workplaces. They are clear, complex, and sometimes confusing, but they are not mysterious.

The variables are not mysterious; they are not buried in the unconscious mind of the family member or worker. The variables can be discovered by rigorous application of common sense. Freud demonstrated that many times, but many professionals either did not read or did not understand that point.

Rigorous application of common sense is within the capability of normal parents or managers or performance analysts. If that is true, why do so many fail to discover the relationships? I cannot say for sure, but I believe the failures are due to a failure to *apply* common sense—either due to emotional involvement or due to listening to too many people spout too much nonsense.

TIPS FOR ANALYSIS

Think for yourself. Question, investigate, organize information, and make recommendations you can defend by explaining clearly and simply how you arrived at them. Technical jargon helps us understand and communicate with others who have mastered the same jargon. But every analyst should become skilled at saying *everything* in the language of the client or in plain English or French or German or Spanish or Japanese or whatever the client speaks. The most skillful analysts can do that while losing very little of the precision of the technical language. They do so by using many examples to clarify meaning.

Important variables—ones I've called "deep structure" variables—in a family or in a business have something in common that makes them surprisingly easy to find. Important variables, almost by definition, relate not to just one thing, but to many things. To find them, look in three places:

- The Mega World, perhaps using the Anatomy of Performance diagram

- The Macro World, perhaps using the Total Performance System diagram and flowcharts drawn in swim-lane format[2]

- The Micro World, perhaps using the Human Performance System diagram

To say the same thing in different words, look for three types of issues:

1. Critical Business or Family Issues, perhaps using the Anatomy of Performance diagram

2. Critical Process Issues, perhaps using flowcharts in swim-lane format and summarized in the Total Performance System diagram format

3. Critical Job/Person Issues, perhaps using the Human Performance System diagram

Look in all three places for all three types of issues. When you have found all three and can explain how the three sets of issues interrelate and interact, you know enough to make a recommendation.

How do you know whether your recommendations are good and understood? They are good and understood only when the client argues with you until every point is clarified and confirmed before agreeing with you.

TIPS FOR ANALYSIS

If the client does not argue or "resist," then worry. It means that the client knows he or she is not going to follow the recommendations or else he or she intends to follow them, but is clueless about how to do it, and does not choose to admit it.

Summary

Two fundamental issues are about relationships and can be managed best if numbers are used:

1. A strategic issue: How can we ensure our family's standard of living and safety, live better with less, yet maintain good relationships with our neighbor, employers, and suppliers?

2. An operations issue: Are we on track toward our goals/objectives/whatever we call them? Are we tracking the right numbers? Not too many, not too few, and at just the right time?

A wise analyst will probe to get information about these two perennial critical family issues during the analysis. Even if the matter under analysis seems to be far removed from these issues, it is not. If the matter under analysis actually is far removed from these issues, it is almost certain to be trivial and not worth pursuing.

Mega World issues are always relevant and always important for strategic planning; however, Mega World issues are often not of immediate concern for routine family matters until after it is too late to deal with them well.

Managers of household finances are often concerned with cost-saving issues. Wilma and Wilber, in their executive roles, might worry about current costs, but their focus is and should be strategic. (That is why executives do not get as excited as managers about cost savings; then, too, most executives have encountered bogus cost-savings data and have learned to be skeptical about it.)

TIPS FOR ANALYSIS

If you want to capture parental attention, focus on critical family issues. That is one way I know I've uncovered a critical family issue during an analysis; critical family issues tend to capture parental attention. Parents listen actively and discuss them energetically. Sometimes an analyst will disagree that the issue is important, and the analyst might be right in some cosmic sense, but the analyst is not the umpire—the one who decides *for* the family.

Many critical family goals or objectives or standards or whatever are set in accord with external realities and constraints. It is important to know about those external realities and constraints when setting performance improvement targets. It is even more important to discuss them with the parents.

An analysis is "good" if and only if it helps parents understand what should be done, why, and how it can be accomplished. Accuracy and completeness are nice.

Analysis tools such as the Total Performance System diagram, the Anatomy of Performance diagram, the Human Performance System diagram, the Organizational Elements Model,[3] cross-functional maps, or the Mission Statement Job Aid are useful because they help the analyst quickly discover, understand, and communicate critical information to clients. Often, but not always, it is helpful to put the information in the diagrams and share and discuss them with the parents.

TIPS FOR ANALYSIS

Making recommendations is a sales process. An analyst can "sell" only what the family will "buy." Some recommendations that cannot be sold, at first, can be sold later if the relationship between the analyst and the family develops well. An analyst should resist the temptation to attribute lack of sales skill to client resistance.

Endnotes

1. Freud, S. (1901). *Psychopathology of everyday life*, translation by A. A. Brill (1914). London: T. Fisher Brill. The book is currently available from several publishers and is available online at http://psychclassics. yorku.ca/Freud/Psycho/intro.htm

2. Many examples of swim-lane format charts can be found in Rummler, G. A., & Brache, A. P. (1995). *Improving performance: How to manage the white space on the organization chart* (2nd Ed.). San Francisco, CA: Jossey-Bass.

3. An example of application of the OEM model can be found in Watkins, R. (2000). Is distance learning right for your organization? http://pignc-ispi.com/articles/distance/isdistance.htm. See also his book in this series, *Performance by Design* (Amherst, MA: HRD Press, 2006.)

Section III
Specifying Improvement Options: Connecting Interventions to the Past, Present, and Future

Here's the way a workplace performance improvement project would be experienced by Wilber, the father in the family system described earlier. Set aside, for the moment, his role in the family; we will focus on his perspective when he is at work.

One Manager's Perspective

Wilber is fully engaged with events at work, events that are already occurring before a new project starts. He sees the executives going off in all directions and doesn't believe any of them really know how the business works. (He might be right; he might be wrong; he just does not know.)

Wilber is also worried about the international scene and about all those politicians in Washington, D. C., and in the Ohio state capital, Columbus, and in Cleveland Heights where he lives. The politicians keep saying bad things about one another; Wilber believes them all. Each one claims to have just the right prescription for the future; Wilber doesn't believe any of them. The prescriptions are all compromises, forced to gain acceptance and "compromised" in the pejorative sense: optimization over multiple time periods is not one of the core competencies of most politicians. What is worse, the compromises all seem to require higher taxes. Wilber doesn't see how he can afford to pay them out of the household budget.

Wilber, even at work, is keenly aware of his role as head of a family. (Wilma, at work, is also keenly aware of *her* role as head of a family.) Wilber vaguely remembers all the trouble he got into when he was just a little older than Tommy is now. He doesn't know whether to worry more about Tommy or about Tammy. Wilber worries about his health. His prostate is okay, but the last article he read on the topic worries him. Besides that, Wilma is getting older, too—well, you get the picture. Wilber has a lot on his plate before this new project starts.

Wilber also remembers several past efforts that people were enthusiastic about. The efforts raised hopes and fears, caused confusion, and went nowhere. He has ideas about pressing business issues that ought to be dealt with and he just isn't sure this new project he is hearing about will do that.

Every New Project

Every performance improvement project occurs in an organization full of Wilbers and Wilmas, all of whom have a lot on their plates. Each has ideas about what would make things better. If the project is a minor one, it will be treated as such and, quite possibly, ignored into a quick demise. If the project is a major one, it will be resisted. That is just the way it is, that is the context in which we specify improvement options!

When I began this type of work many years ago, I came from a fantasy world: In my fantasy, I would do the analysis and come up with a set of recommendations that were overwhelmingly brilliant and immediately implemented. Everyone would be delighted!

The real world was quite different: I was very good at finding relevant variables and creating powerful interventions that went absolutely nowhere.

Many consulting firms do it that way to this day. Maybe it is a core competency for consultants.

But there is a better way. I learned if from my father, a farmer:

1.   Prepare the ground and plant the seeds.

2.   Water, fertilize, and control the weeds.

Prepare the ground from the beginning. Analysis is about finding direction and critical variables. You know that and I know that. What I didn't know at first is that analysis is sales and marketing research as well as analysis.

How you market while doing an analysis is extremely important. Some "analysts" are terrific marketers and poor analysts, successfully selling bad projects. Some "analysts" are terrific analysts and poor marketers, unsuccessful in getting anything beneficial implemented, or so it seems to me.

Fortunately, there is a powerful tactic for building consensus about what to do, how to go about it, and why it should be done:

> Treat each person you talk to as an important
> and valued colleague!

What do you do with important and valued colleagues? Exchange information, try out ideas, learn from them what you do not know, help them learn what their inquiring minds want to know.

The way I make that happen is quite straightforward. As I talk to each person, I capture "Wilber's World" by constructing a Human Performance System diagram for that person. Consider this:

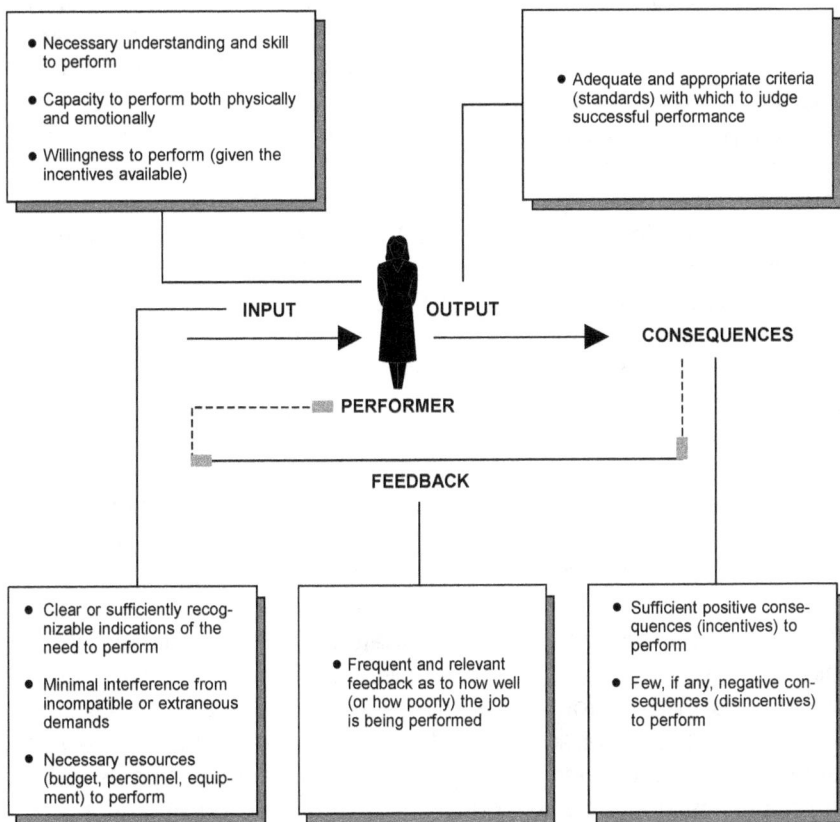

- Necessary understanding and skill to perform

- Capacity to perform both physically and emotionally

- Willingness to perform (given the incentives available)

- Adequate and appropriate criteria (standards) with which to judge successful performance

INPUT   OUTPUT   CONSEQUENCES

PERFORMER

FEEDBACK

- Clear or sufficiently recognizable indications of the need to perform

- Minimal interference from incompatible or extraneous demands

- Necessary resources (budget, personnel, equipment) to perform

- Frequent and relevant feedback as to how well (or how poorly) the job is being performed

- Sufficient positive consequences (incentives) to perform

- Few, if any, negative consequences (disincentives) to perform

Each box lists requirements for what either the person or the organization must bring to the job or task to enable the performer to perform well. As an analyst, I can mentally put Wilma or Wilber or any other performer in the place marked Performer. Then I can ask several questions to get at the information indicated by each box. For example, I might ask: "How do you know when to do this task?

What other tasks or demands compete with doing it? Do you have enough time to do it well or do you have a dozen other things demanding your attention at the same time?" (Box at lower left.) I might ask: "What cues, clues, or feedback do you get that tell you how you are doing?" (Box at lower center.) "What good things happen if you perform well? What bad things happen if you perform well? What good things happen if you perform poorly? What bad things happen if you perform poorly?" (Box at lower right.) I might ask: "How do you know whether you are doing a good job? Are there clear standards of performance? Clear guidelines? Clear examples?" (Box at upper right.) I might ask: "Do you know how to do it well? Do you have the skill to do it well? Do you have the physical ability? The mental ability? Do you like doing it? Do you hate doing it? Are there adequate incentives for doing it or reasons for doing it that make sense to you?" (Box at upper left.) And I would ask very basic questions: "Do you have the tools and materials necessary to do the task well? What else should you have?" (The Input arrow.) "Just what do you accomplish? What is the product or service of your work?" (The Output arrow.)

Want to practice and learn something important as you do? Try making a Human Performance System diagram for at least one of your major areas of responsibility. Then practice by having a conversation with someone, filling it out for that person's job or major responsibility. Do that several times, if you like.

As you do so, you might notice something. Each person's job (or set of tasks) connects to a value-adding process or a support process in the organization. That process links the person's work to the organization as a whole. The value-adding process or support process, of course, fits inside the Anatomy of Performance. When possible, and it is not always possible, I do an HPS for each of the key players in a performance improvement project so that I know exactly where that person fits in the anatomy of performance relevant to the project. I want to know whether the person knows where he or she fits and how to contribute. (Some do, but in my experience, many do not. Those who do not are not stupid; they will resist until they know.) I want to help the person find a fit so that she or he can help and avoid being a misfit and hinder the work. If I find the fit *and benefits of fitting* for a few, I might have the support of those few; it is better to have the support of many.

As my father taught:

1. Prepare the ground and plant the seeds.

2. Water, fertilize, and control the weeds.

Market as you analyze. Chapters 7 and 8 offer concepts and tactics that can help.

Chapter 7
Finding out What Will Work
and with Whom

Overview: Creating Recommendations

This chapter is about tactics for deciding which recommendations to make. There is a huge array of possible recommendations for any performance improvement project. Here is a sample of 14 of them:

1. Train the first line supervisors.

2. Develop the managers.

3. Improve the new product development process.

4. Track the product life cycle and discontinue dying products before they destroy brand identity.

5. Build a job aid for the contract compliance officer.

6. Construct job models for product managers.

7. Fire the COO.

8. Transfer the VP of Finance to the Siberia office.

9. Close the Siberia office.

10. Sell the division before everyone finds out how bad it is.

11. Install an incentive system.

12. Remove an incentive system.

13. Track costs on a timely basis.

14. Immediately hire a new marketing director from outside the company.

You might try listing 12 or 14 or 20 additional recommendations, just to remind yourself that there are *many* possible interventions a performance improvement expert could recommend.

There are also many recommendations for Wilma and Wilber:

1. Send Tommy and Tammy to obedience school or other special camp.

2. Train Wilma and Wilber in the skills of positive discipline.

3. Prepare and implement written development plans for all family members.

4. Inventory the strengths and weaknesses in Wilma's and Wilber's parenting skills, and implement a plan for building on the strengths and eliminating some of the weaknesses.

5. Build job aids for Tommy and Tammy that show them how to do household chores.

6. Build job aids for Tommy and Tammy that show them how to resist peer pressure or make new friends or play nicely with others.

7. Send Tommy to a private boarding school at least 1,000 miles away.

8. Establish an allowance (base pay) for Tommy and Tammy and an incentive system to support their development plans.

9. Prepare and post a list of core values for the family.

10. Play a game in which everyone earns points for "catching others being good."

11. Buy a Doberman for Tammy and a poodle for Tommy and support their efforts to care for the dogs.

12. Play a "happiness game" in which family members earn recognition for doing things others say "helps me be happy."

13. Post the family budget on the refrigerator and have Tommy and Tammy help monitor compliance.

14. Have Wilber and Wilma get marital counseling immediately.

Think about it: Do you suppose every decision maker (whether in a business or a family) is waiting breathlessly for you to present a set of recommendations that he or she has been too dimwitted to think of? Or do you suppose it is more likely that key decision makers will say, "We tried that and it did not work!" or "That might work somewhere, but it would never work here!" or "If we did all that, it still would not solve the problem!"

People do not resist your recommendations because the people are stupid, evil, or just plain contrary. That might happen— I've just never encountered it in 40 years. People resist because they can see the obstacles much more clearly than you can. Consultants often report "findings" in support of each recommendation; it helps a little. But more should be done, especially working with decision makers to identify "implementation obstacles" for major recommendations. I seek, often successfully, to work with clients to develop a set of "implementation plans," complete with timelines and checkpoints and measures. If I have established collaborative relationships during the analysis and then continue the collaboration during implementation planning, there is a good chance that the recommendations will be implemented. The recommendations that get implemented will be ones that the client restates (and "owns") during the collaborative work.

TIPS FOR ANALYSIS

Routinely debrief projects to determine how well the recommendations are implemented and how much they have to be restated. The debriefings can generate a set of "lessons learned" that are very valuable in guiding future work. Link these en-route results with the stated intentions.

It is very rare for recommendations to be implemented exactly as they were written. Why? Because more is learned during implementation. I personally think of "analysis and design" as intellectual exercises that facilitate the real analysis and design. *The real analysis and design occurs during implementation.*

Interventions Related to Critical Business Issues or Critical Family Issues

Here is something important to know about systems, be they business organizations or families or whatever: Everything is connected to everything else. That connectedness is, at minimum, an important property. Some people consider it a defining property.

Here is something else worth knowing: The more important a recommended intervention is, the more aspects of the system it will be connected to. That means that, even if the recommendation "should" be implemented, it will be resisted. (Systems operate to remain stable; change feels like destabilization to the people involved; resisting destabilization is something that people do every day, thank goodness! Homeostatic mechanisms are important for survival and form the context for any change effort.)

Please consider this conclusion for performance improvement analysts:

If you want to avoid resistance, avoid doing anything connected to a

- Critical Business Issue
- Critical Process Issue
- Critical Job Issue

I have sometimes gotten a sinking feeling in a project because I was *not* encountering resistance. If there is no resistance, the project is probably *not* connected to a Critical Issue, and quite likely it is not worth doing! Why would any sane person resist a pointless project? Especially if the person has seen many other pointless projects begin with enthusiasm and then fade away?

One reason executives seem uninterested in otherwise brilliant recommendations: The recommendations are of marginal importance if they are not connected to Critical Business Issues!

TIPS FOR ANALYSIS

Search for Critical Business Issues or Critical Family Issues. If you want to help make a significant and positive impact, be sure that your recommendations support the actions related to the CBI or CFI. If you want to maintain a low profile and have little impact, avoid Critical Issues.

Motivations and Incentives for Decision Makers

Some actors, given a few lines to read, will ask, "What's my motivation?" That is, "What is my character trying to accomplish with these lines? Avoid responsibility? Ingratiate? Seduce? Embarrass? Expose a powerful enemy? Establish credibility? What?" Some performance improvement analysts, given a request for an analysis or intervention might ask, "What's the motivation behind the request? What important opportunity or threat does it relate to?" The motivation behind requests varies, but the serious performance improvement professional will seek out requests related to Critical Issues.

TIPS FOR ANALYSIS

Whatever the motivation behind the request, the findings and recommendations should address it. What did the request for a proposal say was wanted? What did people say they wanted when the project first began? Is the motivation organizational improvement? Enhancement of status of an executive or department? Spending extra money that is in the budget so that the money is not swept up and used elsewhere? Do you suspect the stated reasons for the request do not tell the whole story? Have you asked questions that would help you discover "hidden" motives? For better or worse, such motivations are relevant to your task of making recommendations that will be implemented. (And yes, I have discovered motivations I could not ethically support and have, sometimes, been able to walk away from such projects. Maybe I should have always walked away.)

If the motivation for the request—or a likely outcome of the project—is improvement of organizational performance through addressing one or more Critical Business Issues, then the project has a high potential pay-off.

TIPS FOR ANALYSIS

My training in psychology did not prepare me to recognize a Critical Business Issue even when I encountered one. I had to rely on colleagues with business sense. I could have done all right by asking executives and managers, "Is this a Critical Business Issue?" Some executives and some managers might answer the question right away. Some might know the answer, but will not trust you enough to answer directly and clearly. Some might hope to learn the answer from the analysis. Similarly, some might not understand the question. But if an executive or manager asks, "What do you mean?" the answer goes something like this: "I mean an issue that comes up often in discussion of how to achieve strategic or operational goals. Is it an issue that is highly relevant to threats and opportunities? Is it an issue that keeps you awake at night? Is it an issue that impacts current and future revenue streams or cost issues? Is it an issue that either adds value to or subtracts value from society?"

The motivations of the people who request the project and of the people who will be involved in implementing the recommendations are very important. But, and this is also important, the motivations will usually be partially aligned with the best interests of the organization. (Otherwise, the people would not still be in the organization.) The partial alignment provides a starting point to build a consensus about the truth of the findings and the potential of the recommendations!

As the analysis proceeds, the analyst will develop and gain agreement about exactly what is in the best interests of the organization, not just in the abstract, but as it relates to the forthcoming recommendations. Every decision made and action taken as a result of the recommendations will be made by a human being, usually one with organizational responsibilities *and* family responsibilities. The more clearly the recommendations support specific organizational responsibilities, the easier it will be for a decision maker to fulfill the organizational responsibilities and, we hope, do so without setting aside family responsibilities.

Interventions Related to Critical Process Issues

We know something very important about the solutions to Critical Business Issues:

The solutions will involve "reengineering" a critical process.

This is because the problems related to the issues should not only be solved, for now, but the solution should involve making as sure as possible that whatever is "fixed" stays fixed. The solution should include recommendations about ensuring that the improved performance does not drift back toward poor performance.

Please take this as a working hypothesis:

Solving problems related to Critical Business Issues and keeping them from recurring will require making changes in important work processes.

Why? Because a Critical Business Issue will always, or almost always, involve improving important numbers. Numbers such as:

1. The number of customers. That number implicates the processes for acquiring, serving, and maintaining relationships with customers.

2. The number and size of projects completed, the profit margin on each project or each product line, the total revenues by product or service line, the total costs by product or service line.

3. The rate of inventory turn.

4. The turnover of all employees or the turnover within key employee categories such as "sales executive" or "information systems designers" or "quality engineers" or "production engineers" or whatever.

5. The numbers and dollar amounts of returned products, numbers of key customers, and dollar amounts of revenue from each customer category.

Each number or set of numbers implicates specific processes for doing the work related to "making the numbers."

Please notice something else about the numbers and related processes: The work related to important numbers will always, or almost always, cut across organizational boundaries. That means that no one person or department is the "culprit"—the source of the problem. No one person or department holds the solution to the problem.

TIPS FOR ANALYSIS

Projects often come to us from one department, possibly Production Scheduling or New Product Development or Human Resources or whatever. That means that the ones requesting the analysis do not have their hands and heads and hearts connected to the variables that must be altered to solve the problem or create the solution or develop the brand new thing the client asks for. Consider asking questions like these a lot:

- Who else could influence the outcome?
- Who might be helped or harmed if the problem is solved?
- Who might be helped or harmed if the problem is not solved?
- How should I move forward to involve those people?

You probably know that important organizational issues have many stakeholders and that stakeholders can innocently or purposefully work at cross-purposes. The performance analyst must work with a variety of stakeholders and work to align the interests of each stakeholder with the goals of the project.

TIPS FOR ANALYSIS

A way to do that is to draw flowcharts of important processes, showing how each stakeholder is connected to an important process that impacts the overall organizational goal.

Consider this: If an issue is muddled, throwing a bunch of words at it is unlikely to clarify it much. Why? Because the important words will *often have multiple definitions* and *always have multiple connotations*. As long as each person "sends" messages using words alone, the messages will be "received" with meanings attached that are quite different from what the sender intended. That will be true even if all persons involved agree to use just one of the words to describe the muddle.

That is just the way it is because of the way human beings learn to use words. And it is why "clarifying and confirming" is part of many communications courses. Clarifying and confirming is necessary. Furthermore, it takes a lot of clarifying and confirming to reach a consensus on anything. And it goes much faster if the clarifying and confirming are done with pictures and diagrams and specific examples. That is not news to any expert in communications or instructional design; such experts can provide both theory and examples that would convince almost anyone that pictures and diagrams help a lot.

That is why "is-maps" (charts showing how something is currently) are so valuable in an analysis. Draw a flowchart, and ask people to tell you what it means to them and then to tell you whether or not you have captured, accurately, how the work *is actually* done. Such analysis almost always generates surprises, arguments, and statements such as these: "That's what people say they do, but actually, it is not done that way." "That's a better way of doing it than what we are doing now; let's change!" Remember that the flowcharts, by themselves, do not mean anything. Many people do not even understand them unless you walk them through a few times.

TIPS FOR ANALYSIS

A flowchart, like sentences and paragraphs and essays, has a "grammar"—a structure. The grammar or structure might not be understood. Hence, walking people through them a few times is good advice. Asking "What does this mean to you?" is a very good thing to do. Confirm and clarify!

The Critical Process Analysis is completed when people agree on:

1. How something is being done now

2. How it should be done in the future

3. That the "should" way differs from the "is" way

TIPS FOR ANALYSIS

Speak the language of the client, but don't lose the rigor of what must be communicated and accomplished. Many technical people speak the language of numbers and flowcharts reasonably well. Many people who work, let us say, in education or education-like departments in business do not do numbers and flowcharts readily. Consider starting with whatever language they use. Almost everyone is familiar with "To Do" lists or lists of steps or forms to fill out. In my experience, the grammatically challenged exhortation to "start where the client is at" is a good practice. But leaving the client muddled is not. Clarify and confirm your way to consensus, doing it in whatever way you can. My bet is that, over some time period, you will find yourself more and more using numbers and diagrams and flowcharts and such.

Interventions Related to Critical Job Issues

Who are the people who perform "critical jobs" anyway?

They are everyone who is trying to make the status quo work—who is trying to do the work the way the work is done now. They are anyone and everyone who will be involved in doing the work the way the project says it should be done.

What is a Critical Job Issue?

A Critical Job Issue is familiar ground for experts in "training needs analysis." It is the ground covered by Gilbert's Behavior Engineering Model (BEM)[1] and/or Geary Rummler's Human Performance System diagram.[2] It is any issue connected with ensuring that critical performers can and will perform well. A few questions can direct the analysis to the right matters: "Could the person do it if his or her life depended upon it?" "Could the person do it if he or she knew how?" (Ability, Motivation, and Knowledge and Skill) "Could the person do it if he or she had the right tools and materials?" "The right information and guidance?" "The right incentives?" "The right feedforward and the right feedback?" (Environmental Support)

TIPS FOR ANALYSIS

Do not fall into the trap of "if you have a hammer, everything should be pounded." Many of us, over the years, have been tasked with analyzing until we find knowledge or skill deficits in some category of employees such as first line supervisors, widget makers, and so on. We were then tasked with running a training program tailored to that set of deficits for that category of employees. We were *not* tasked with improving performance, but with overcoming knowledge and skill deficits. Our challenge now is to work ourselves out of the old tasking (do training) and into a new tasking: improve performance.

Changing job performance reliably requires us to deal with more than the one cell in the Behavioral Engineering Model and/or more than one category in the Human Performance System diagram. The BEM and HPS are "maps" of essentially the same territory. We must deal with all the variables that influence performance. We must look at guidance and goals and feedback and task interference and the like. We must deal with ensuring that individual performance is aligned with process goals and with organizational goals.

A caveat: Please allow me to say a word or two about the topic of motivation as in "motivating workers" or "motivating decision makers." Long before Sigmund Freud unleashed the concept of unconscious motivation and the mysterious workings of the Id, Ego, and SuperEgo, people have been concerned with the mysteries of why people do what they do. Psychologists, psychiatrists, motivation theorists, and educated persons have been especially intrigued by the mysteries of motivation. As an analyst for performance improvement, you must be attuned to the variables influencing performance. Ignoring important variables, be they associated with the personality, attitudes, feelings, or motivations of performers, would be foolishly myopic.

But focusing on mysterious motivations is something that no leading motivational theorist advocates or does.

Leading motivational theorists seek to take the "mystery" out of motivation[3]; they seek to make the mysterious commonplace. Those who succeed take the mystery out of motivation. They do so by identifying variables in the person's interaction with the person's environment that "explain" the motivation. They do so by identifying variables!

When we analyze for performance improvement, we seek variables that we can modify to better support the performance that adds value in organizations. Some of the variables, such as those involved in incentives, pay systems, feedback systems, goal setting, management systems, management techniques, consensus building, peer influence, conflict resolution, and the like, are the very variables motivation theorists focus on.

However, some variables focused on by motivation theorists are ignored in the sense that they are not variables the performance improvers can change. For example, I cannot recommend a solution that requires changing someone's personality, family history, medical history, psychiatric history, or the like. I happen to be licensed to practice clinical psychology, but most of my clients— the people who would implement my recommendations—are not. Therefore, I must make recommendations that are legal and humane and that can be applied in an organizational setting by people who do not have a clinician's license.

Does that limit my effectiveness (and yours) as performance analysts? You might say so. I prefer to think that it is not a limitation, but a constraint. It is a constraint that I believe is healthy and wise. It is a constraint like driving on the road to get through a swamp. It is a constraint like the constraint of recommending things that are sound business practices. It enhances my competence. I can make recommendations that make the work environment a healthy and supportive environment—an environment that supports the best people have to offer and does not support the worst they have to offer.

Summary

This chapter—and much of this book—is about finding what will work to change and *improve* performance. Finding what will work is about finding:

- Critical Business Issues
- Critical Process Issues
- Critical Job Issues

Finding Critical Business Issues is about finding ways to add value to the Macro World of customers and suppliers and investors and the Mega World of the economic, social, and physical environment.

Finding Critical Process Issues is about finding better ways to add the value, specifying tactics, and strategies for doing specific things well, now and on an ongoing basis.

Finding Critical Job Issues is about supporting the performance of everyone involved: the executives who set direction, the managers who organize the resources, and all the people who do all the thousands of tasks involved.

Each person involved has an essential job. The performance of each job (and, thereby, each process and the managing of all the variables related to Critical Business and Process and Job Issues) must be managed on an ongoing basis.

Making recommendations to be implemented is a technical and a social activity. The intelligent cooperation of every person is desirable; the intelligent cooperation of most of them is essential.

Making recommendations that will be implemented is an effort that involves winning the "hearts and minds" of the people involved. No performance improvement effort will be perfect, but every performance improvement effort should be performed as intelligently and collaboratively as possible.

The entire process of analysis is, like marketing research, an attempt to find value-adding performances that will be "bought with gusto" by the people involved.

Endnotes

1. The BEM is described fully in this book: Gilbert, T. (1996). *Human competence: Engineering worthy performance.* Amherst, MA & Washington, D. C.: HRD Press, Inc. & The International Society for Performance Improvement. (A tribute reissue of Gilbert, 1978). One of the six cells in the BEM is labeled "Motives," but please know that all six cells describe variables related to motivation.

2. There is a generic HPS diagram in Chapter 3 of this book. The HPS is described in Rummler, G. A., & Brache, A. P. (1995). *Improving performance: How to manage the white space on the organization chart* (2nd Ed.). San Francisco, CA: Jossey-Bass. The book contains several examples of the HPS.

3. Good summaries of many of the major approaches to motivation can be found in Pinder, C. C. (1997). *Work motivation in organizational behavior.* Englewood Cliffs, NJ: Prentice Hall. Available in university libraries and on Amazon.com. See also Richard Gerson's book in this series, *Achieving High Performance* (Amherst, MA: HRD Press, 2006.)

Chapter 8
Specifying the Tactics:
Identifying the Mix of Interventions

Overview: Focusing the Confusion

Performance analysis was invented to avoid two very common pitfalls: prematurely jumping to a solution and analysis paralysis.

Historically, most performance improvement pioneers had a strong background in science. Endless analysis is the bread and butter of science. We habitually analyzed issues that few of our clients thought were important such as the immediate interpersonal consequences of actions. We often failed to analyze issues that clients thought were important such as the effect of an intervention on cash flow or on strategy implementation. The net result was that our analysis bias was in constant conflict with the jump to solution bias of clients.

Although "jumping to a solution" was readily accepted by many clients, it mired us in the swamp of incompetence too much of the time. Adding one or two or many "new and improved" interventions to a set of pet solutions is popular with marketers. (Marketers like to announce new services regularly.) But it does not serve the performance improvement marketplace well in the long run.

Fortunately, we learned how to avoid both the "jump to a solution" and the "analysis paralysis" approaches to performance improvement. How? By learning how to focus performance analysis sharply and on the right issues.

TIPS FOR ANALYSIS

The road to efficient performance analysis is to seek answers to good questions—the right questions for the setting and purpose. We are getting quite good at knowing the right questions and are making significant improvement in organizing the answers to guide action. But asking the wrong questions still occurs.

Most performance analysts know about several different interventions: training, work redesign, process improvement, coaching,
incentives, culture changes, establishing new or different goals,
improving new product development procedures, improving super-
visory or management procedures, and many more. But analysts
should be careful to ask the right questions about these interventions:

1. Which ones should we use?
2. When?
3. How?
4. Of all the things we know how to do, which
   should we do now?

These seem like good questions. **But they are not.** They are
all "jump to solution" questions. They are simply wrong-headed.
They focus on "our solutions" not the clients' issues. Clients sometimes sense this and, correctly, resist it. We might have just the
hammer the client might use to "fix" a problem, but hammer-centric
analyses are not the kind for competent performance analysts to
do.

Here is a question that leads to a better line of questioning:

Of all the things that could be done, which should we do or
partner with others to do so that we get the results we
want?

A good line of questioning should not have us seeking "solutions" that are already in our tool kit. It opens the possibility that
there are other tools out there that we can collaborate with others to
use. It also reminds us that any useful tool can be misused.

A comprehensive performance improvement effort will have
several parts and use a variety of tools:

- Think about project management tools and Gantt Charts
  and the like.

- Think about a stakeholder matrix that lists every stakeholder
  or stakeholder group and the commitments, benefits, and
  risks to each from doing the performance improvement
  project.

- Think about Kaufman's Organizational Elements Model,
  Rummler's Anatomy of Performance diagram, and my Total
  Performance System diagram.

The easy solutions have already been tried before clients (internal or external) ask for help. We must think, not of discovering *the* solution or *the* cause of a performance deficit or *the* success strategy, but of gaining credibility and support. We are attempting to collaborate with clients to find a set of changes that will support high levels of performance.

Our performance analysis task is not one of discovering solutions or causes or opportunities, though all that happens. It is an educational task—a task of helping clients learn what should be done, how, why, when, by whom, and how well. It is a task of learning, with the client, about a set of manageable interventions that will add value to multiple stakeholders.

Managing the Set of Interventions

It is easy to discover an array of potentially valuable interventions. Think about your tendency, my tendency, and the clients' tendencies to "jump to solutions" and leverage that tendency.

TIPS FOR ANALYSIS

Here is one way to do that: Ask everyone in sight, "What do you think should be done? What have you tried in the past? How did that work? Let us call what you think should be done your hypothesis. Is that okay, or are you absolutely sure it would solve all of our problems? What are some other hypotheses?"

When I say "everyone in sight," I mean every stakeholder. That is, I mean every decision maker and everyone who might impact the performance and be impacted by the performance. Each one is likely to have a solution in mind, which, if you do not consider, will reduce your credibility.

Your task is not merely to "identify solutions," but to help the client discard many possible solutions that might already have support. A competent analyst will help clients discard "jumped to" solutions and do it in ways that satisfy the persons who believed those solutions were the ones to use. Your task is to align stakeholders with an array of tactics that will be very likely to yield the results the stakeholders want.

TIPS FOR ANALYSIS

1. Make a stakeholder matrix that has "Stake-holders" listed as rows and "Stakes," "Hypotheses," "Reasons to support," "Reasons to resist" and such items as the columns. Whatever else you do during the analysis, fill in the matrix. It will give you an enormous amount of guidance as you work with clients to figure out implementation strategies, tactics, guidelines, benchmarks, and measures of success and failure. (I rarely share the stakeholder matrix with clients, but I think I should do so more often.)

2. Make another stakeholder matrix with "Stake-holders" listed as rows. Use the columns to capture competing duties or responsibilities or pressures. For example, in a typical organization, every stakeholder will be involved in multiple "initiatives" before you ever start. These other initiatives are making demands on the stake-holders. Some initiatives will compete with your interventions; others might support or facilitate your interventions. You are likely to find that some important aspect of your interventions is already being attempted and should be leveraged to support your intervention.

3. Make another stakeholder matrix with "Stake-holders" listed as rows. Use a column to specify what each stakeholder should do to support the total intervention package. Use another column to specify what each stakeholder *could* do to oppose the intervention package or some key part of it. Use other columns to specify when each stake-holder will be contacted, by whom, and to what end. Be sure to be in contact with stakeholders frequently enough to renew agreements, remind them of the purpose(s) of the effort, and get input. Especially get input. A good way to position both planned and unplanned contacts with stake-holders is by saying, "Here's what has been happening and what the current thinking is... Where are we going wrong?"

In other words, please make use of the best techniques of human relations and project management that you can. If you have a favorite way to manage projects, use it as a checklist to see if the project management techniques in use in the organization will do the job at least as well. Use the client's techniques as much as possible.

Linking the Set of Interventions to Routine Management Processes

Thinking only about "implementation" is a very popular way to fail. Focusing only on implementation and not thinking about a longer time period almost ensures that an intervention has, at best, transitory benefits. If your intervention were to do a heart transplant, you would not be foolish enough to ignore the possibility of a delayed rejection of the heart. It is the same with an intervention or set of interventions.

Organizations are very effective at delayed rejection of interventions. That is one reason today's popular intervention tends to join other interventions in the trash heap of history.

TIPS FOR ANALYSIS

Figure out how to "hardwire" the new ways of doing things into the current and routine management practices and the culture of the organization. Failure to do so is like implanting a mouse heart into an elephant or vice versa.

Your task is to provide answers to this question:

How will this "new" thing look and feel when it is an "old" thing?

Will it be reviewed periodically to see how it is working? To see if it is still beneficial? To see how to improve it? To see how to replace existing/competing practices with the practices supported by the intervention? To smooth out the operation and improve efficiency so that the client can phase out temporary and special funding?

TIPS FOR ANALYSIS

Do a competition and facilitation analysis. Think about everything that is happening that might compete. Think about everything that is happening that might help. Guesstimate how much additional support is required to get the intervention package working smoothly and then to convert it to routine operation.

One reason the performance analyst should be thinking ahead is that if the intervention is directed at a Critical Business Issue, we do not seek temporary results. We seek results that will endure as long as the business issue is important. Consider questions such as these:

- If the issue relates to new product development, how long will the organization benefit from a good new product development process?

- If the issue relates to customer satisfaction, how long will the organization benefit from good customer relations practices?

- If the issue relates to improving financial management, how long will the organization benefit from good financial management practices?

The answers, of course, have two parts: First, the issues will be important for a long long time (unless the organization dies). Second, the specific actions taken now will not be the right actions at some point in the (near) future. If you are dealing with a Critical Business Issue, the process for dealing with that issue *must remain in place and/or be continually improved.* For example, the customer relations process will remain important; the specific tactics used will, necessarily, change from time to time. Or the technologies employed in the new product development process will change, perhaps rapidly.

TIPS FOR ANALYSIS

Years ago, a group of us working out of the University of Michigan Center for Programmed Learning for Business annoyed many people in the training industry with this slogan: "If you can't maintain it, don't train it!" Another way of saying that is "If they will not do it after training, training them to do it adds cost, not value." More generally, the slogan means that temporary "fixes" are rarely worth the cost of the "fix." Cars come with spare tires, crutches are useful to a person with a broken leg, and temporary heroics are valuable on occasion. Spare tires, crutches, and the like can support solutions and are worth considering. Such thinking is good, *but it does not justify offering training that doesn't transfer. That would be even less effective than providing adjustable wrenches to save costs in going metric.*

Here's another annoying slogan: "If you cannot maintain the performance, your intervention will have, at best, short-lived positive effects."

The slogan, per se, is too wordy to be memorable, but treatment packages that deal only with "change" and not with "maintenance" or "routine operations" tend to fail and leave a lingering memory that you were heavily involved in a project that did not work. (We—a group at the University of Michigan Center for Programmed Learning—actually used "If you can't maintain it, don't train it" as a teaching point. We liked it a lot; it annoyed clients a lot.)

TIPS FOR ANALYSIS

One way to gain support for designing intervention packages that work is to focus your performance improvement work on Critical Business Issues. Two other supplementary ways are: "Focus your performance improvement work on Critical Process Issues" and "Focus your performance improvement work on Critical Job Issues."

You probably know why it is important to focus on all three—
and to keep the implementation focused on all three—but I will tell
you anyway. If it is focused on a Critical Business Issue, it *probably*
will be worth the cost. If it is focused on a Critical Process Issue, it
will *probably* be seen as important organizationally. If it is focused
on one or more Critical Job Issues, it will *probably not* be seen as
focused on finding fault with the persons doing the jobs now. To say
that in a different way:

1. If it is focused on a CBI, it will be seen as worth doing and
    have leadership support.

2. If it is focused on a CPI, it will be seen as possible to do
    and have managerial support.

3. If it is focused on CBIs and CPIs and CJIs, it will be less
    likely to be seen as threatening the well-being of specific
    people who would otherwise seek to block the project.

Three other points worth making:

1. Executives often bemoan the fact that people in the
    organization muddle around doing many things that might
    seem urgent, but that add more confusion than value.
    They want support of managers and all the people. "Don't
    people know that this is a business? That we have to
    satisfy shareholders and customers? That we live in a
    competitive environment?"

2. Managers often bemoan the fact that each executive
    pushes a flavor of the month and that few executives
    understand how the organization really works. They want
    support of executives and all the people. "Don't executives
    know that they do not have their act together—that they
    give out conflicting signals? Don't they know that they
    punish us if we attend to the wrong signal? Don't they
    know that we have work to do and people to keep going?
    Don't workers know that little bits of stupidity add up to
    major costs and customer dissatisfaction?"

3. Workers often bemoan muddled leadership and
    management, and believe that neither executives nor
    managers know how the work should be done and that
    both executives and managers insist on doing things that

hinder rather than help. "Don't people know what customers want and that *we* are the ones who provide it—or could if some of the bureaucratic nonsense was removed? Don't they know that some people get ahead by playing management's games and others don't get ahead because they do the job?"

All three—executives, managers, and workers—are on target with their complaints. That is something to be aware of and leverage, if possible, when selling a proposed course of action. Aligning executives, managers, and workers is an ongoing organizational problem. It always is and always will be. Each project you do can improve the situation or make it worse.

TIPS FOR ANALYSIS

1. Every executive's and every manager's role keeps changing. The current role makes sense only with a view to the past and almost never makes sense with a view to the future! An executive's job or a manager's job will only make sense when his or her job is aligned with CPIs and CBIs.

2. Focusing on CBIs, CPIs, and CJIs will be seen by some as ignoring "the human element" such as personality conflicts, motivation, and the like. But if you were to study the literature on how "the human element" manifests itself in organizations, you might come to agree with a conclusion I've reached after reading dozens of books, several hundred research studies, and working in the field for more than 40 years. The approach I am recommending here focuses *directly* on "the human element" by focusing on the variables that influence the health and well-being and best interests of *each* and *all* of the stakeholders. The approach *deals with the variables directly;* it does not just label and discuss the human variables.

Measurement and Management Systems

Excellence does not occur consistently by accident. Performance must be measured and managed. If the Critical Job Issue is consistently producing "good widgets," the number, quality, and cost of "good widgets" must be measured. The measures are not necessary because some accountant or industrial engineer is anal-retentive, but because without them, neither the widget maker nor the manager of widget making nor the person in charge of widget sales or widget customer relations can know how well the organization is performing. Without the measures, people cannot take corrective action intelligently when it is called for, and they cannot make continuous improvements.

TIPS FOR ANALYSIS

The measures are a necessary means of communication in the workplace. No amount of communications training can improve communications if the right numbers are missing, the wrong numbers are being used, and/or the right numbers are not available to the right people at the right time.

Somewhere in the midst of any analysis, you will find that the wrong numbers are attended to, the right numbers are missing, and/or the numbers are not available to the right people at the right time. Trust me. Or, better yet, try to find an instance that proves me wrong—an instance in which everyone has the right numbers at the right time and in the right form to perform intelligently. ("Everyone" includes the persons who designed or who administer the compensation system, the training systems, the work flow, and the like.)

The implication for implementation: If the intervention package does not include ensuring that at least a few very fundamental numbers reach the right people at the right time (to serve as feedback) *and* will continue to do so, the package will fail to achieve the results desired. Similarly, unless the right numbers reach the right people at the right times and in the right forms during the implementation, the implementation will be suboptimal.

TIPS FOR ANALYSIS

1. Making sure that everyone knows what information everyone must have to perform intelligently might sound like a very difficult task. It is. But the tactics for making it happen are straightforward. Just keep asking this question: "How will you know if X is happening the way it should?" (for example, "How will you know that customer satisfaction is improving?" "That quality trends are within control limits and headed in the right direction?" "That you are doing the tasks well that your boss wants you to do?"). Asking the question repeatedly will help keep the question in the forefront. Then, top it off by asking this question repeatedly: "What measures can we put in place that ensure that people know how well the work is being done?" The answers help you collaborate with others to design a measurement and management system, without which the intervention package is likely to fail.

2. The tactics for designing the measurement and management system are essentially the same as the tactics for what was once called "developmental testing" in training or programmed learning and the tactics for what is often called "alpha testing" in other fields.

3. Developmental testing and alpha testing are methods that work in the design of anything complex, including the design and implementation of performance improvement intervention sets. If you or I were omniscient, we could develop the set of interventions some other way. And if you or I were omnipotent, we could get our beautifully designed interventions implemented. But since I am neither, I've never been able to do it. Perhaps you have had similar experiences.

Summary

The key to developing a set of successful performance improvement interventions is to ensure that there is a measurement and management system that:

- Links the several components of the intervention strategy *to the CBI, the CPI, and the relevant CJIs*

- Links the intervention to routine management procedures (even if those procedures must be improved as part of the intervention package)

That is, the key is to have a set of interventions that:

1. Will be implemented

2. Will favorably impact measures of the CBI, the CPI, and the CJIs

3. Can be maintained and continually improved through organizational measurement and management systems that are implemented as part of the performance improvement effort

Failing that, you or I might aspire to develop interventions that do #1 and #2 but not #3 and develop good relationships with people who can hire us again to help "fix" things when they fall apart.

Appendix A
Analysis Tools

This appendix contains blank copies of four of the tools used in this book. The four tools are ones that are useful in determining what to do and why for performance improvement projects.

There is a brief commentary on the use of each tool. The tools are:

1. Job Aid for Goal Statements/Mission Statements

2. Human Performance System Diagram

3. Total Performance System Diagram

4. Anatomy of Performance Diagram

Job Aid:
Goal Statements/Mission Statements

Please understand that terms such as *goals, objectives, missions, purposes* and the like are not used the same way by everyone. (Not a surprise, is it?) I tend to use whatever terminology the client uses. The exception is when I am working with a company that has several divisions or when I am working with a professional or business association. Then I strongly recommend that those involved in the analysis—as analysts or as consumers—define their terms collaboratively and, thereby, use a terminology that everyone will understand.

The following tool can be used to quickly arrive at a "pretty good" mission statement or statement of purpose or statement about just why we are doing all this.

One way I use the tool is to ask small groups of people to:
1. Individually, answer the questions listed on the tool
2. Discuss and agree on the answers
3. Write a short statement summarizing the agreements

It takes about 3 minutes for the individual work, about 10 to 15 minutes for the discussion/agreement, and another 10 minutes to craft the statement.

If you—the analyst—know Gilbert's Performance Engineering Matrix, especially the Philosophical Level, you can readily lead people to the Philosophical Level. And if you know Kaufman's Organizational Elements Model (OEM), you can lead people toward a statement that recognizes the Mega World.

Keep in mind that merely writing the statement does not make it real. It is used as part of a consensus-building procedure. The writers must "make meaning" by linking activities to the parts of the statement and attaching measures to the various parts of the statement.

The tool is quite useful in getting a "roughly right" statement that can be refined and improved. Some analysts try to get it "exactly right." I understand why they do that, but getting the words "exactly right" is difficult and, even though they are "exactly right" on the surface, shared meanings will not develop until later on in a project.

Here is the tool I call a Job Aid for Generating Mission Statements:

Job Aid for Generating Mission Statements

Question 1.   What do we call the system we are analyzing?

_____

_____

Question 2.   What is the main activity of the system? What are the major outputs/products/services?

_____

_____

Question 3.   What are the products/services good for? What values or standards are supported?

_____

_____

Question 4.   Who receives and benefits from the products or services? How do they benefit?

_____

_____

Question 5.   How does society and the world in general benefit?

_____

_____

Job Aid:
Human Performance System Diagram

The diagram, commonly used by Geary Rummler and his colleagues, helps the analyst understand a specific job or task and determine the support necessary if the person doing it is to perform well. As you look at the diagram below, much of it will seem like common sense to you. Who in his right mind would expect someone to perform well if the person did not have the tools to do the job? Who in her right mind would expect someone to perform a moderately complex or creative task without receiving feedback on work in progress? But I must tell you that in doing the analysis hundreds of times and talking with others who have done it *many* times, I have yet to discover an instance in which the HPS was found to be "all there." Every intervention has, at some point or other, involved improving the HPS.

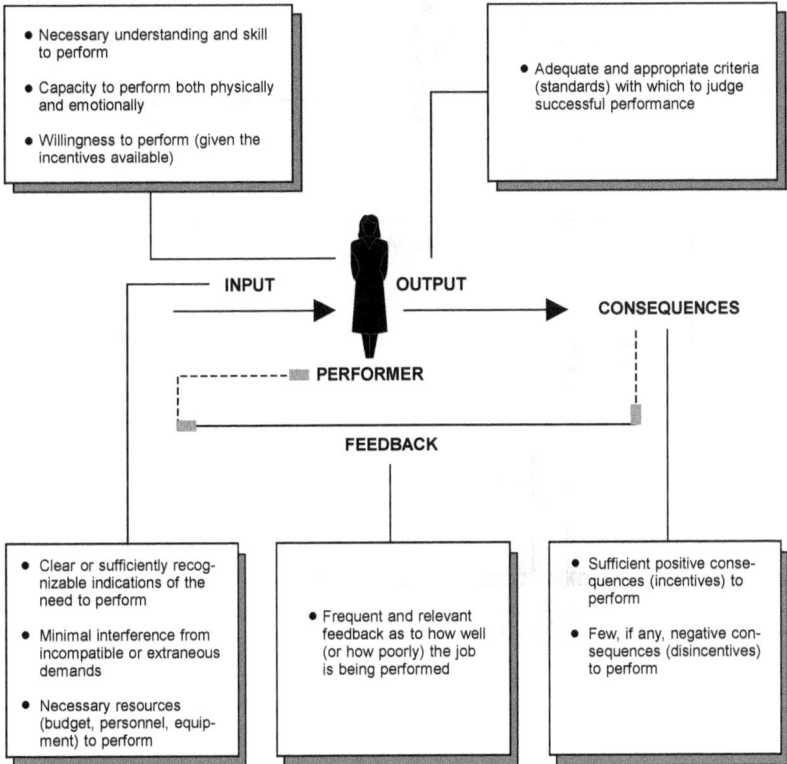

- Necessary understanding and skill to perform
- Capacity to perform both physically and emotionally
- Willingness to perform (given the incentives available)

- Adequate and appropriate criteria (standards) with which to judge successful performance

INPUT OUTPUT CONSEQUENCES

PERFORMER

FEEDBACK

- Clear or sufficiently recognizable indications of the need to perform
- Minimal interference from incompatible or extraneous demands
- Necessary resources (budget, personnel, equipment) to perform

- Frequent and relevant feedback as to how well (or how poorly) the job is being performed

- Sufficient positive consequences (incentives) to perform
- Few, if any, negative consequences (disincentives) to perform

If you are familiar with Tom Gilbert's Behavior Engineering Model (BEM) or my Total Performance System (TPS) diagram, you will be able to see that the Human Performance System diagram is quite similar to either of those tools. You can use analysis tools such as these (see blank HPS diagram below) to focus communication with clients and choose the one that, for whatever reason, is easiest for the client to understand and discuss intelligently.

Human Performance System

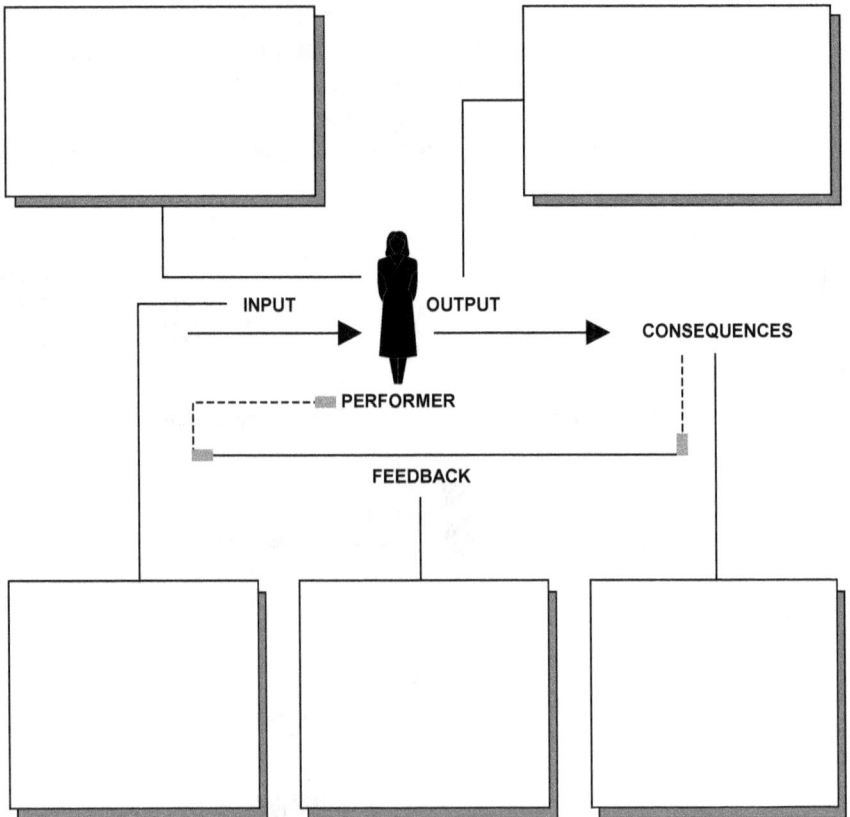

INPUT   OUTPUT

CONSEQUENCES

PERFORMER

FEEDBACK

Job Aid:
Total Performance System Diagram

The Total Performance System Diagram is "total" because it captures the essential ingredients in an adaptive system—a system that can take corrective action while working to achieve goals *and* take intelligent action to change goals to adapt to new threats or opportunities.

The diagram was invented by Dale Brethower, Karen Brethower, George Odiorne, and Geary Rummler more than 40 years ago. It was used to show people that what went on "outside the box" is important. One of the first uses was to illustrate that the "box," the training room, added value if and only if it served purposes outside itself—outside the training room. Thus, objectives such as "Students will learn a, b, and c..." were considered important but insufficient. Objectives such as "Students will learn a, b, and c and then perform to standard on the job" were emphasized. Similarly, an organization such as the Reading Improvement Service at a major university must serve purposes "outside itself." For example, objectives such as "Students will double their reading speed while increasing or maintaining comprehension" was not enough. "Students will improve reading skills and use them to learn better or faster in their university courses" was the goal. The diagram was to call attention to customers and other stakeholders, the territory that Kaufman refers to as Mega. In use, it put major emphasis on adding value to customers and little or no emphasis on "tomorrow's child."

I usually attach numerals to the diagram for ease of reference: 1. Goal Statement, 2. External Feedback Loop, 3. Receiver, 4. Output Arrow, 5. Internal Feedback Loop, 6. Processing (often labeled "Processing System"), and 7. Input Arrow. The words *Total Performance System* are typically replaced by the name of the system being described, e.g., "The University of Michigan."

Total Performance System

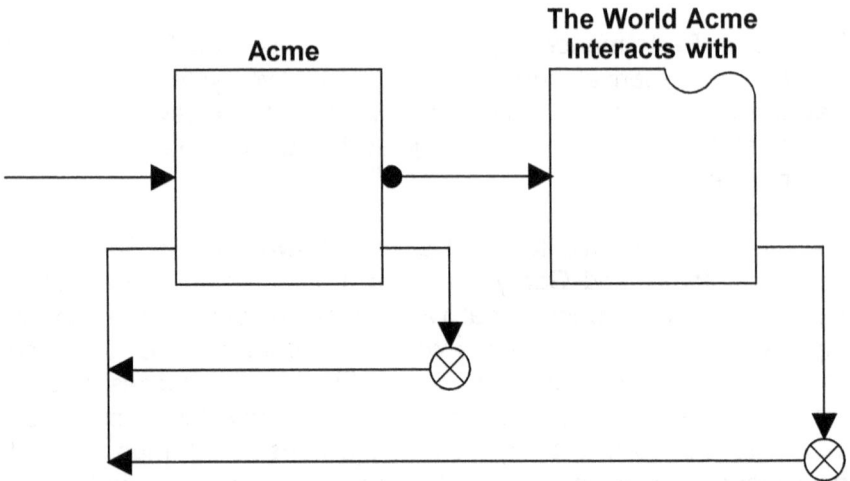

Goal Statement: _____

Feel free to practice using the tool a few times by describing organizations you know about, such as Acme Landscaping or Bob's Grocery or Francine's Folly or General Motors.

Job Aid:
Anatomy of Performance Diagram (AOP)

Geary Rummler and his colleagues have been using the Anatomy of Performance (AOP) diagram in a variety of formats for many years. A blank AOP form is included on the next page.

Examples of the diagram are shown in the book to describe Acme Landscaping and to describe the Wilma/Wilber/Tammy/Tommy family. Another example of the Anatomy of Performance diagram is shown on page 171. It has a slightly different format than the ones for Acme and for Wilma et al.

I use the AOP format when I want to get started, but not pull out a lot of detail. This format reminds the client that there are four classic categories of inputs (money, materials, people, and know-how). It does not go into the sources of these inputs and does not divide the input "money" into "capital" and "revenue." The Marketplace box helps the analyst emphasize that for-profit and not-for-profit organizations are both money generators and products/services generators. It is quite true that for both analyst and client, "the devil is in the details." The AOP provides a context for understanding and prioritizing those details.

If a client asks me to work on an internal process, I will first emphasize those boxes and then ask about the Marketplace as we try to figure out what to measure in order to measure "performance improvement."

If I do not know which version of the diagram I should use, I start with any version and, as the client and I work to fill it in, we would decide which issues are the Critical Business Issues and work from there.

Systemic View: Your Organization

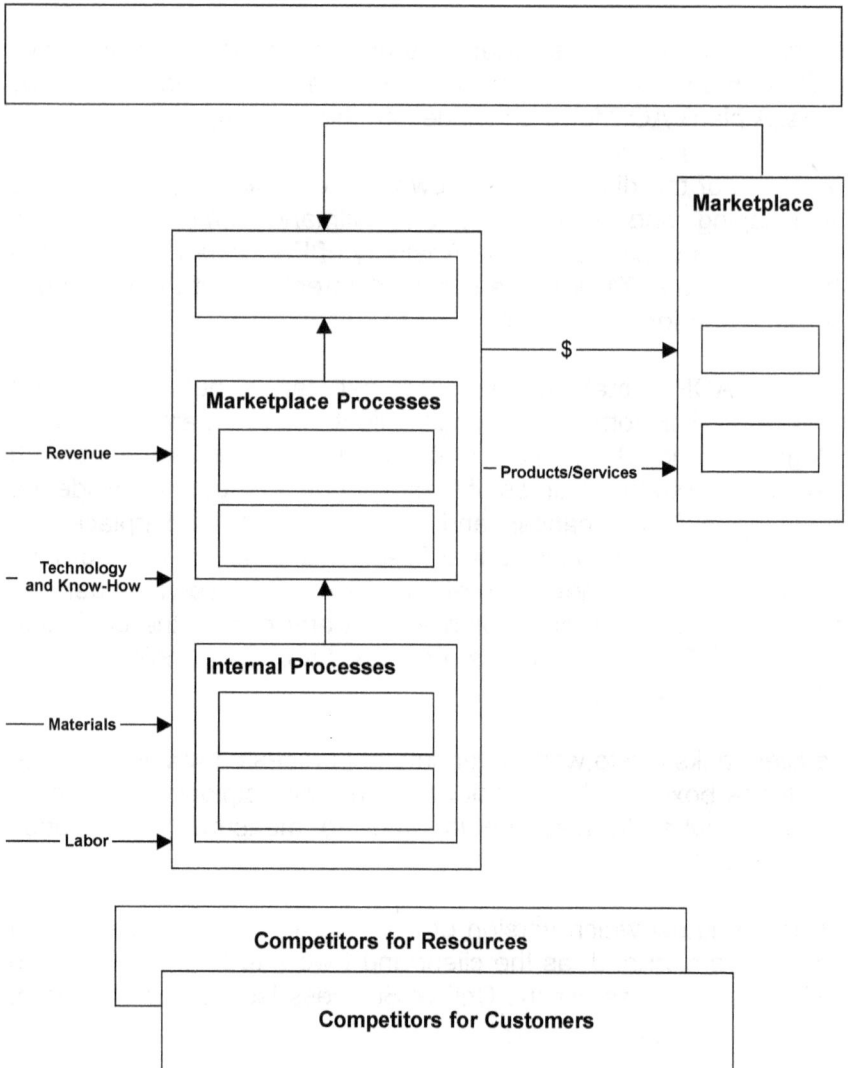

Systemic View: Any Organization

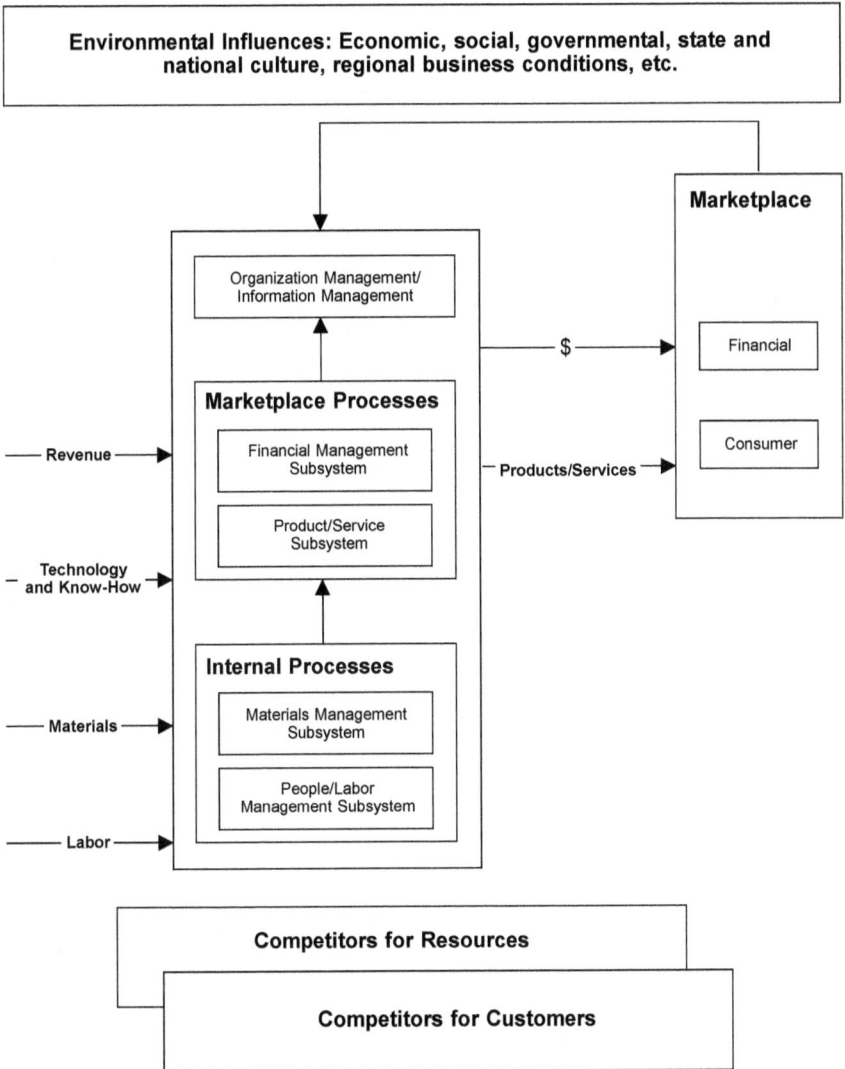

Environmental Influences: Economic, social, governmental, state and
national culture, regional business conditions, etc.

Marketplace

Organization Management/
Information Management

$ ⟶ Financial

Marketplace Processes

—— Revenue ⟶

Financial Management
Subsystem

⌐ Products/Services

Consumer

Product/Service
Subsystem

— Technology
and Know-How ⟶

Internal Processes

—— Materials ⟶

Materials Management
Subsystem

People/Labor
Management Subsystem

—— Labor ⟶

Competitors for Resources

Competitors for Customers

Glossary of Terms[1]

This glossary includes definitions already provided. This is a complete summary of important terms and concepts.

System, systems, systematic, and systemic: related but not the same

system approach: Begins with the sum total of parts working independently and together to achieve a useful set of results at the societal level, adding value for all internal and external partners. We best think of it as the large whole and we can show it thus:

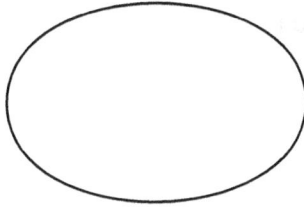

systems approach: Begins with the parts of a system—subsystems—that make up the "system." We can show it thus:

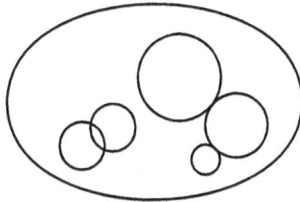

It should be noted here that the "system" is made up of smaller elements, or subsystems, shown as bubbles embedded in the larger system. If we start at this smaller level, we will start with a part and not the whole. So, when someone says they are using a "systems approach" they are really focusing on one or more subsystems, but they are unfortunately focusing on the parts and not the whole. When planning and doing at this level, they can only assume that the payoffs and consequences will add up to something useful to society and external clients, and this is usually a very big assumption.

systematic approach: An approach that does things in an orderly, predictable, and controlled manner. It is a reproducible process. Doing things, however, in a systematic manner does not ensure the achievement of useful results.

systemic approach: An approach that affects everything in the system. The definition of *the system* is usually left up to the practitioner and may or may not include external clients and society. It does not necessarily mean that when something is systemic it is also useful.

Now, let's turn to other strategic thinking and planning terms.

AADDIE model: The ADDIE model with the vital function of Assessment added to the front of it.

ADDIE model: A contraction of the conventional instructional systems steps of Analysis, Design, Development, Implementation, and Evaluation. It ignores or assumes a front determination through assessment of what to analyze, and it also assumes that the evaluation data will be used for continuous improvement.

change creation: The definition and justification, proactively, of new and justified as well as justifiable destinations. If this is done before change management, acceptance is more likely. This is a proactive orientation for change and differs from the more usual *change management* in that it identifies in advance where individuals and organizations are headed rather than waiting for change to occur and be managed.

change management: Ensuring that whatever change is selected will be accepted and implemented successfully by people in the organization. Change management is reactive in that it waits until change requirements are either defined or imposed and then moves to have the change accepted and used.

comfort zones: The psychological areas, in business or in life, where one feels secure and safe (regardless of the reality of that feeling). Change is usually painful for most people. When faced with change, many people will find reasons (usually not rational) for why not to make any modifications. This gives rise to Tom Peter's (1997) observation that "it is easier to kill an organization than it is to change it."

constraints: Anything that will not allow one to meet the results specifications. These might arise from many sources, including not enough resources, insufficient time, political pressures, and the like.

costs-consequences analysis: The process of estimating a return-on-investment analysis before an intervention is implemented. It asks two basic questions simultaneously: what do you expect to give and what do you expect to get back in terms of results? Most formulations do not compute costs and consequences for society and external client (Mega) return on investment. Thus, even the calculations for standard approaches steer away from the vital consideration of self-sufficiency, health, and well-being (Kaufman & Keller [1994]; Kaufman, Keller, & Watkins [1998]; Kaufman [1998, 2000]).

criteria: Precise and rigorous specifications that allow one to prove what has been or has to be accomplished. Many processes in place today do not use rigorous indicators for expected performance. If criteria are "loose" or unclear, there is no realistic basis for evaluation and continuous improvement. Loose criteria often meet the comfort test, but don't allow for the humanistic approach to care enough about others to define, with stakeholders, where you are headed and how to tell when you have or have not arrived.

deep change: Change that extends from Mega—societal value added—downward into the organization to define and shape Macro, Micro, Processes, and Inputs. It is termed *deep change* to note that it is not superficial or just cosmetic, or even a splintered quick fix. Most planning models do not include Mega results in the change process, and thus miss the opportunity to find out what impact their contributions and results have on external clients and society. The other approaches might be termed *superficial change* or *limited change* in that they only focus on an organization or a small part of an organization.

desired results: Ends (or results) identified through needs assessments that are derived from soft data relating to "perceived needs." *Desired* indicates these are perceptual and personal in nature.

ends: Results, achievements, consequences, payoffs, and/or impacts. The more precise the results, the more likely that reasonable methods and means can be considered, implemented, and evaluated. Without rigor for results statements, confusion can take the place of successful performance.

evaluation: Compares current status (what is) with intended status (what was intended) and is most commonly done only after an intervention is implemented. Unfortunately, *evaluation* is used for blaming and not fixing or improving. When blame follows evaluation, people tend to avoid the means and criteria for evaluation or leave them so loose that any result can be explained away.

external needs assessment: Determining and prioritizing gaps, then selecting problems to be resolved at the Mega level. This level of needs assessment is most often missing from conventional approaches. Without the data from it, one cannot be assured that there will be strategic alignment from internal results to external value added.

hard data: Performance data that are based on objectives and independently verifiable. This type of data is critical. It should be used along with "soft" or perception data.

Ideal Vision: The measurable definition of the kind of world we, together with others, commit to help deliver for tomorrow's child. An Ideal Vision defines the Mega level of planning. It allows an organization and all of its partners to define where they are headed and how to tell when they are getting there or getting closer. It provides the rationality and reasons for an organizational mission objective.

Inputs: The ingredients, raw materials, and physical and human resources that an organization can use in its processes in order to deliver useful ends. These ingredients and resources are often the only considerations made during planning without determining the value they add internally and externally to the organization.

internal needs assessment: Determining and prioritizing gaps, then selecting problems to be resolved at the Micro and Macro levels. Most needs assessment processes are of this variety (Watkins, Leigh, Platt, & Kaufman [1998]).

learning: The demonstrated acquisition of a skill, knowledge, attitude, and/or ability.

learning organization: An organization that sets measurable performance standards and constantly compares its results and their consequences with what is required. Learning organizations use performance data, related to an Ideal Vision and the primary mission objective, to decide what to change and what to continue—it learns from its performance and contributions. Learning organizations may obtain the highest level of success by strategic thinking: focusing everything that is used, done, produced, and delivered on Mega results—societal value added. Many conventional definitions do not link the "learning" to societal value added. If there is no external societal linking, then it could well guide one away from the new requirements.

Macro level of planning: Planning focused on the organization itself as the primary client and beneficiary of what is planned and delivered. This is the conventional starting and stopping place for existing planning approaches.

means: Processes, activities, resources, methods, or techniques used to deliver a result. Means are only useful to the extent that they deliver useful results at all three levels of planned results: Mega, Macro, and Micro.

Mega level of planning: Planning focused on external clients, including customers/citizens and the community and society that the organization serves. This is the usual missing planning level in most formulations. It is the only one that will focus on societal value added: survival, self-sufficiency, and quality of life of all partners. It is suggested that this type of planning is imperative for getting and proving useful results. It is this level that Rummler refers to as *primary processes* and Brethower calls the *receiving system.*

Mega thinking: Thinking about every situation, problem, or opportunity in terms of what you use, do, produce, and deliver as having to add value to external clients and society. Same as *strategic thinking.*

methods-means analysis: Identifies possible tactics and tools for meeting the needs identified in a *system analysis.* The methods-means analysis identifies the possible ways and means to meet the needs and achieve the detailed objectives that are identified in this Mega plan, but does not select them. Interestingly, this is a comfortable place where some operational planning starts. Thus, it either assumes or ignores the requirement to measurably add value within and outside the organization.

Micro-level planning: Planning focused on individuals or small groups (such as desired and required competencies of associates or supplier competencies). Planning for building-block results. This also is a comfortable place where some operational planning starts. Starting here usually assumes or ignores the requirement to measurably add value to the entire organization as well as to outside the organization.

mission analysis: Analysis step that identified: (1) what results and consequences are to be achieved; (2) what criteria (in interval and/or ratio scale terms) will be used to determine success; and (3) what are the building-block results and the order of their completion (functions) required to move from the current results to the desired state of affairs. Most mission objectives have not been formally linked to Mega results and consequences, and thus strategic alignment with "where the clients are" are usually missing (Kaufman, Stith, Triner, & Watkins [1998]).

mission objective: An exact, performance-based statement of an organization's overall intended results that it can and should deliver to external clients and society. A mission objective is measurable on an interval or ratio scale, so it states not only "where we are headed" but also adds "how we will know when we have arrived." A mission objective is best linked to Mega levels of planning and the Ideal Vision to ensure societal value added.

mission statement: An organization's Macro-level "general purpose." A mission statement is only measurable on a nominal or ordinal scale of measurement and only states "where we are headed" and leaves rigorous criteria for determining how one measures successful accomplishment.

need: The gap between current results and desired or required results. This is where a lot of planning goes "off the rails." By defining any gap as a *need,* one fails to distinguish between means and ends and thus confuses what and how. If *need* is defined as a gap in results, then there is a triple bonus: (1) it states the objectives (What Should Be), (2) it contains the evaluation and continuous improvement criteria (What Should Be), and (3) it provides the basis for justifying any proposal by using both ends of a need—What Is and What Should Be in terms of results. Proof can be given for the costs to meet the need as well as the costs to ignore the need.

needs analysis: Taking the determined gaps between adjacent organizational elements, and finding the causes of the inability for delivering required results. A needs analysis also identifies possible ways and means to close the gaps in results— needs—but does not select them. Unfortunately, *needs analysis* is usually interchangeable with *needs assessment.* They are not the same. How does one "analyze" something (such as a need) before they know what should be analyzed? First assess the needs, then analyze them.

needs assessment: A formal process that identifies and documents gaps between current and desired and/or required results, arranges them in order of priority on basis of the cost to meet the need as compared to the cost of ignoring it, and selects problems to be resolved. By starting with a needs assessment, justifiable performance data and the gaps between What Is and What Should Be will provide the realistic and rational reason for both what to change as well as what to continue.

objectives: Precise statement of purpose, or destination of where we are headed and how we will be able to tell when we have arrived. The four parts to an objective are (1) what result is to be demonstrated, (2) who or what will demonstrate the results, (3) where will the result be observed, (4) what interval or ratio scale criteria will be used? Loose or process-oriented objectives will confuse everyone (c.f. Mager [1997]). A Mega-level result is best stated as an objective.

outcomes: Results and payoffs at the external client and societal level. Outcomes are results that add value to society, community, and external clients of the organization. These are results at the Mega level of planning.

outputs: The results and payoffs that an organization can or does deliver outside of itself to external clients and society. These are results at the Macro level of planning where the primary client and beneficiary is the organization itself. It does not formally link to outcomes and societal well-being unless it is derived from outcomes and the Ideal (Mega) Vision.

paradigm: The framework and ground rules individuals use to filter reality and understand the world around them (Barker [1992]). It is vital that people have common paradigms that guide them. That is one of the functions of the Mega level of planning and outcomes so that everyone is headed to a common destination and may uniquely contribute to that journey.

performance: A result or consequence of any intervention or activity, including individual, team, or organization: an end.

performance accomplishment system (PAS): Any of a variety of interventions (such as "instructional systems design and development," quality management/continuous improvement, benchmarking, reengineering, and the like) that are results oriented and are intended to get positive results. These are usually focused at the Micro/Products level. This is my preferred alternative to the rather sterile term *performance technology* that often steers people toward hardware and premature solutions (Kaufman [1999, 2000]).

Processes: The means, processes, activities, procedures, interventions, programs, and initiatives an organization can or does use in order to deliver useful ends. While most planners start here, it is dangerous not to derive the Processes and Inputs from what an organization must deliver and the payoffs for external clients.

products: The building-block results and payoffs of individuals and small groups that form the basis of what an organization produces and delivers, inside as well as outside of itself, and the payoffs for external clients and society. Products are results at the Micro level of planning.

quasi-need: A gap in a method, resource, or process. Many so-called "needs assessments" are really quasi-needs assessments since they tend to pay immediate attention to means (such as training) before defining and justifying the ends and consequences (Watkins, Leigh, Platt, & Kaufman [1998]).

required results: Ends identified through needs assessment, which are derived from hard data relating to objective performance measures.

restraints: Possible limitations on what one might use, do, and deliver. Restraints serve as a type of performance specification.

results: Ends, products, outputs, outcomes—accomplishments and consequences. Usually misses the outputs and outcomes.

soft data: Personal perceptions of results. Soft data is not independently verifiable. While people's perceptions are reality for them, they are not to be relied on without relating to "hard"—independently verifiable—data as well.

strategic alignment: The linking of Mega-, Macro-, and Micro-level planning and results with each other and with Processes and Inputs. By formally deriving what the organization uses, does, produces, and delivers to Mega/external payoffs, strategic alignment is complete.

strategic thinking: Approaching any problem, program, project, activity, or effort by noting that everything that is used, done, produced, and delivered must add value for external clients and society. Strategic thinking starts with Mega.

tactical planning: Finding out what is available to get from What Is to What Should Be at the organizational/Macro level. Tactics are best identified after the overall mission has been selected based on its linkages and contributions to external client and societal (Ideal Vision) results and consequences.

wants: Preferred methods and means assumed to be capable of meeting needs.

What Is: Current operational results and consequences. These could be for an individual, an organization, and/or for society.

What Should Be: Desired or required operational results and consequences. These could be for an individual, an organization,
and/or society.

wishes: Desires concerning means and ends. It is important not to
confuse *wishes* with *needs.*

Making Sense of Definitions and Their Contribution to a Mega Perspective

Here are some ground rules for strategic thinking and planning:

1. System Approach ≠ Systems Approach ≠ Systematic
   Approach ≠ Systemic Approach

2. Mega-Level Planning ≠ Macro-Level Planning ≠ Micro-Level
   Planning

3. System Analysis ≠ Systems Analysis

4. Means ≠ Ends

5. Hope ≠ Reality

6. Outcome ≠ Output ≠ Product ≠ Process ≠ Input

7. There are three levels of planning: Mega, Macro, and
   Micro, and three related types of results: Outcomes,
   Outputs, Products.

8. Need is a gap in results, not a gap in Process or Input.

9. Needs Assessment ≠ Needs Analysis (nor front-end
   analysis or problem analysis)

10. Strategic Planning ≠ Tactical Planning ≠ Operational
    Planning

11. Change Creation ≠ Change Management

Endnote

1.   Based on Kaufman, R., & Watkins, R. (2000, April). Getting serious
     about results and payoffs: We are what we say, do, and deliver.
     Performance Improvement, 39 (4), 23–31.

About this Series

Defining and Delivering Successful Professional Practice—HPT in Action

This is the second of six books to define and deliver measurable performance improvement. Each volume defines a unique part of a fabric: a fabric to define, develop, implement, and continually improve human and organizational performance success. In addition, the series relates to the professional standards in the field.[1]

Why This Series?

Human and Organizational Performance Accomplishment—some call the field HPT (Human Performance Technology)—is of great interest to practitioners and clients alike who intend to deliver successful results and payoffs that are based on research, ethics, and solid concepts and tools. The author of each book provides a practical focus on a unique area, and each book is based on 10 principles of professional contribution.

Each book "stands alone" as well as knits with all the others. Together they:

1. Define the field of HPT and performance improvement based on the principles of ethical and competent practice.

2. Provide specific guidance on six major areas of professional practice.

3. Are based on a common framework for individual and organizational performance accomplishment.

4. Reinforce the principles that drive competent and ethical performance improvement.

There is a demand for an integrated approach to Human and Organizational Performance Accomplishment/Human Performance Technology. Many excellent books and articles are available (some by the proposed authors), but none covers the entire spectrum of the basic concepts and tools, nor do they give the integrated alignment or guidance that each of these six linked books provides.

This series is edited by Roger Kaufman (Ph.D., CPT), Dale Brethower (Ph.D.), and Richard Gerson (Ph.D., CPT).

The six books and the authors are:

Book One: *Change, Choices, and Consequences: A Guide to Mega Thinking and Planning.* Roger Kaufman, Professor Emeritus, Florida State University, Roger Kaufman & Associates, and Distinguished Research Professor, Sonora Institute of Technology

Book Two: *Performance Analysis: Knowing What to Do and Why.* Dale Brethower, Professor Emeritus, Western Michigan University and Research Professor, Sonora Institute of Technology

Book Three: *Performance by Design.* Ryan Watkins, Associate Professor, George Washington University, Senior Research Associate, Roger Kaufman & Associates, and former NSF Fellow

Book Four: *Achieving High Performance.* Richard Gerson, Ph.D., CPT, Gerson Goodson, Inc.

Book Five: *Implementation and Management of Solutions.* Robert Carlton, Senior Partner, Vector Group

Book Six: *Evaluating Impact: Evaluation and Continual Improvement for Performance Improvement Practitioners.* Ingrid Guerra-López, Ph.D., Assistant Professor, Wayne State University and Associate Research Professor, Sonora Institute of Technology as well as Research Associate, Roger Kaufman & Associates

How This Series Relates to the Professional Performance Improvement Standards

The following table identifies how each book relates to the 10 Standards of Performance Technology[2] (identified by numbers in parentheses ( ) pioneered by the International Society for Performance Improvement (ISPI).[3] In the table on the following page, an "X" identifies coverage and linking, and "✓" indicates major focus).

This series, by design, goes beyond these standards by linking everything an organization uses, does, produces, and delivers to adding measurable value to external clients and society. This six-pack, then, builds on and then goes beyond the current useful criteria and standards in the profession and adds the next dimensions of practical, appropriate, as well as ethical tools, methods, and guidance of what is really required to add value to all of our clients as well as to our shared society.

	Focus on Results (1)	Take a System Approach (2)	Add Value (3)	Partner (4)	Needs Assessment (5)	Performance Analysis (6)	Design to Specification (7)	Selection, Design, & Development (8)	Implementation (9)	Evaluation & Continuous Improvement (10)
Book 1	✓	✓	X	✓	✓	X	X	X		✓
Book 2	X	✓	✓	X		✓	✓			X
Book 3	X	X	X			✓	✓	✓		X
Book 4	X	X	X	X		✓	X	✓	✓	X
Book 5	X	✓	✓	✓		✓	✓		✓	✓
Book 6	✓	✓	✓	X	✓				X	✓

All of this will only be useful to the extent to which this innovative practice becomes standard practice. We invite you to the adventure.

Roger Kaufman, Ph.D., CPT
Dale Brethower, Ph.D.
Richard Gerson, Ph.D., CPT

Endnotes

1. The Standards of Performance Technology developed by the International Society for Performance Improvement, Silver Spring, Maryland.

2. Slightly modified.

3. Another approach to standardization of performance are a set of competencies developed by the American Society for Training and Development (ASTD), *ASTD Models for Human Performance Improvement,* 1996, which are more related to on-the-job performance.

About the Author

Dale Brethower, Ph.D., has degrees from the University of Kansas (AB), Harvard University (AM), and the University of Michigan (Ph.D.). He is the recipient of the Outstanding Achievement award in organizational behavior management from the Association for Behavior Analysis International and the Honorary Member for Life award from the International Society for Performance Improvement (ISPI). He was a visiting scholar at Keio University in Japan in 1994. Dale has authored or co-authored 8 books and more than 50 published papers. He is a licensed clinical psychologist and has a certificate in the fundamentals of Rational-Emotive Counseling. Dale has been a consultant more than 30 years with a client list including 43 public sector and 23 private sector organizations, primarily in the United States. He has served on the staff of the Evaluation Center (Western Michigan University), the Center for Effective Learning (Cleveland State University), and the Center for Programmed Learning for Business, the Center for Research on Language and Language Behavior, the Center for Research on Learning and Teaching, and the Reading Improvement Service (all at the University of Michigan). He served two terms on the board of directors of the ISPI and is a former president of the ISPI. He served as a board member and as president of the North Central Reading Association and served on advisory boards for the Institute for Rational Living and for Ronningen Research and Development.

Dale is a member of the advisory board of the Performance Systems Analysis area of the Cambridge Center for Behavioral Studies. He is a consulting editor for the *Performance Improvement Quarterly* and guest editor for the *Journal of Organizational Behavior Management.* He is a professor emeritus of Psychology, Western Michigan University, and a visiting research professor at the Technological Institute of Sonora, Mexico.

www.ingramcontent.com/pod-product-compliance
Lightning Source LLC
Chambersburg PA
CBHW070400200326
41518CB00011B/1997